Shropshire, Staffordshire and West Midlands

ROGER NOYCE

COUNTRYSIDE BOOKS
NEWBURY BERKSHIRE

First published 2005

COUNTRYSIDE BOOKS
3 Catherine Road
Newbury, Berkshire

To view our complete range of books,
please visit us at
www.countrysidebooks.co.uk

ISBN 1 85306 904 3

Photographs by Margaret Noyce
Maps by the author

Designed by Peter Davies, Nautilus Design
Produced through MRM Associates Ltd., Reading
Typeset by Techniset Typesetters, Newton-le-Willows
Printed by Arrowsmith, Bristol

Contents

INTRODUCTION

WALKS IN SHROPSHIRE

1. **Bishop's Castle:** The Boar's Head (4½ miles) 9
2. **Oswestry:** The Eagles Inn (6 miles) 12
3. **Stiperstone:** The Stiperstones Inn (5 or 7½ miles) 15
4. **Ruyton XI Towns:** The Talbot Inn (4 miles) 18
5. **Ellesmere Lakes:** The Red Lion (6 miles) 21
6. **Craven Arms:** The Stokesay Castle Hotel (3½ miles) 24
7. **Carding Mill Valley:** The Yew Tree (5½ miles) 27
8. **Uffington:** The Corbet Arms (6½ miles) 30
9. **Ludlow:** The Church Inn (7 miles) 33
10. **Whitchurch:** The Old Town Hall Vault (5 miles) 36
11. **Wenlock Edge:** The George and Dragon (3½ miles) 39
12. **Little Wenlock:** The Huntsman (7 miles) 42
13. **Cleehill:** The Kremlin (8 miles) 45
14. **Eardington, near Bridgnorth:** The Halfway House Inn (4½ miles) 48
15. **Cheswardine:** The Wharf Tavern (4 miles) 51

WALKS IN STAFFORDSHIRE

16. **Norbury:** The Junction Inn (7 miles) 54
17. **Kinver:** The Vine (4½ miles) 57
18. **Hill Top:** The Rose & Crown (4½ miles) 60
19. **Brewood:** The Admiral Rodney (5 miles) 63
20. **Wombourne:** The Plough Inn (7½ miles) 66
21. **Barlaston:** The Duke of York (3½ miles) 69
22. **Cannock Chase:** The Barley Mow (7 miles) 72
23. **Meerbrook:** The Lazy Trout (7½ miles) 75
24. **Abbots Bromley:** The Goat's Head (3 miles) 78
25. **Dimmingsdale:** The Ramblers Retreat (4½ miles) 81

Contents

WALKS IN STAFFORDSHIRE (continued)

26. Ellastone: The Duncombe Arms (6 miles) 84
27. Grindon: The Cavalier Inn (5½ miles) 87
28. Whittington: The Swan (4¼ miles) 90
29. Alrewas: The Crown (3¼ miles) 93
30. Tatenhill: The Horseshoe (6 miles) 96

WALKS IN THE WEST MIDLANDS

31. Penn: The Barley Mow (3 miles) 99
32. Leasowes Park: The Black Horse (4¼ miles) 102
33. Dudley: The Dudley Port (5¼ miles) 105
34. Walsall Wood: The Boatman's Rest (5½ miles) 108
35. Cannon Hill Park: The Selly Park Tavern (3½ miles) 111
36. Sutton Park: Toby Carvery (7 miles) 114
37. Solihull: The Masons' Arms (7 miles) 117
38. Marston Green: The Little Owl (4½ miles) 120
39. Berkswell: The Bear Inn (5 miles) 123
40. Coventry: The Flying Standard (3 miles) 126

PUBLISHER'S NOTE

We hope that you obtain considerable enjoyment from this book; great care has been taken in its preparation. Although at the time of publication all routes followed public rights of way or permitted paths, diversion orders can be made and permissions withdrawn.

We cannot, of course, be held responsible for such diversion orders and any inaccuracies in the text which result from these or any other changes to the routes nor for any damage which might result from walkers trespassing on private property. We are anxious though that all details covering the walks are kept up to date and would therefore welcome information from readers which would be relevant to future editions.

The simple sketch maps that accompany the walks in this book are based on notes made by the author whilst checking out the routes on the ground. However, for the benefit of a proper map, we do recommend that you purchase the relevant Ordnance Survey sheet covering your walk. The Ordnance Survey maps are widely available, especially through booksellers and local newsagents.

Introduction

The sparkle of a river meandering through a scenic valley, a visit to a typical old English pub in a picturesque setting, the enchantment of a colourful narrowboat passing under an ornate canal bridge, a walk over green hills where panoramic views take one's breath away – these are a few of the wonderful experiences that can be enjoyed in abundance in Shropshire, Staffordshire and the West Midlands.

The walks in this book offer you the opportunity to sample all of these delights as well as suggesting a number of interesting excursions to complement your outing. You can stroll by a river, along a canal towpath, or take up the challenge of a more testing hill-climb. Whatever type of circuit you select, you will have the chance to admire some of the finest scenic views and historic buildings in England and complete a perfect day out at a friendly pub. There can be few greater pleasures in life than to visit a pub after a good walk.

In Shakespeare's day, Birmingham was a small English market town set amid forests and common land, although even then it was noted for its large number of smiths making a wide range of iron goods. The Industrial Revolution (Ironbridge Gorge in Shropshire claims to be its birthplace) saw the expansion of trades and crafts, and Queen Victoria proclaimed Birmingham a city. Birmingham was at the centre of the industrialized world in the 18th century, and a large number of canals were built to distribute the many

On the Shropshire Way

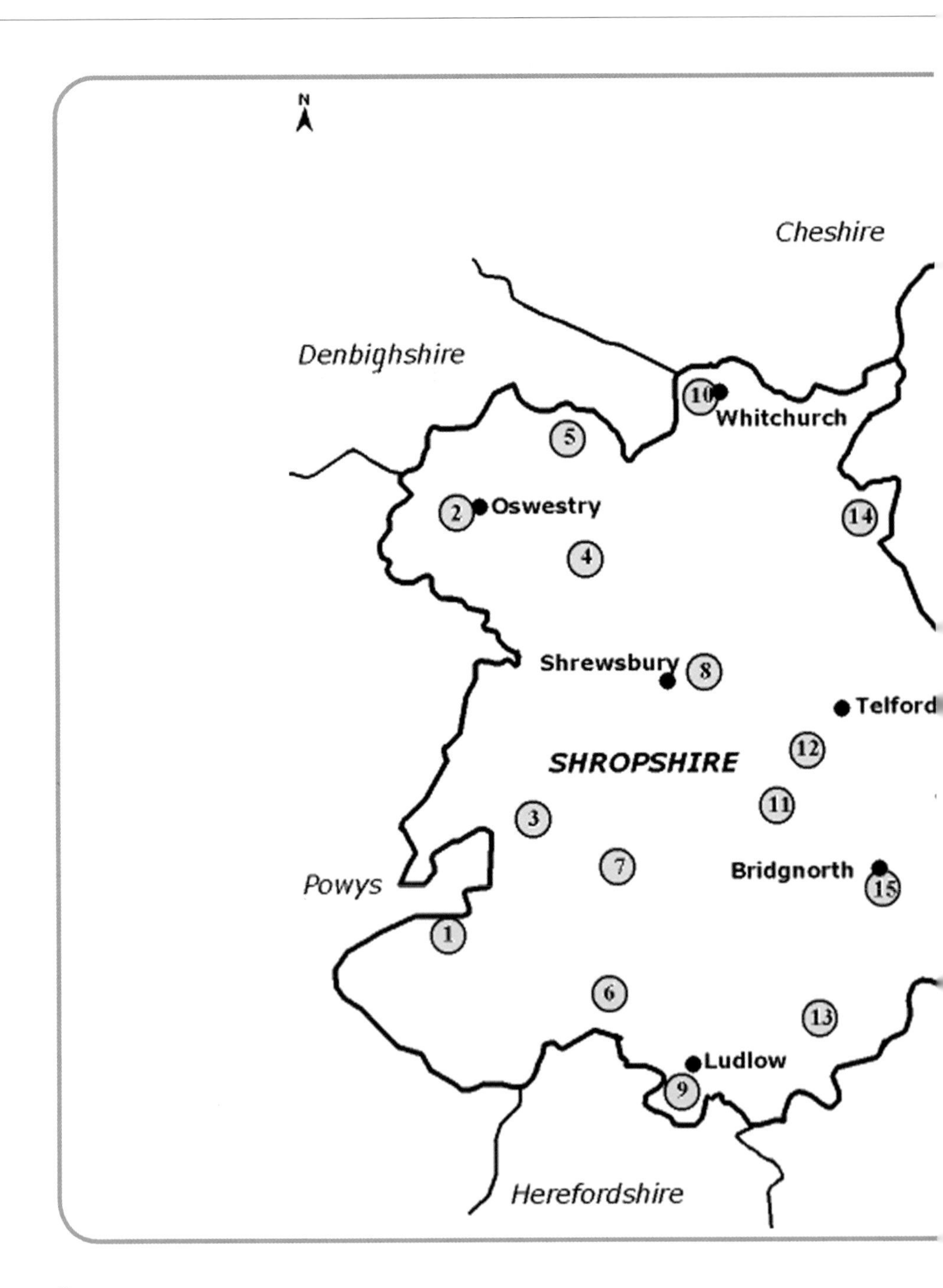
N
Cheshire
Denbighshire
10
Whitchurch
5
2
Oswestry
14
4
Shrewsbury
8
Telford
12
SHROPSHIRE
11
3
7
Bridgnorth
15
Powys
1
6
13
Ludlow
9
Herefordshire

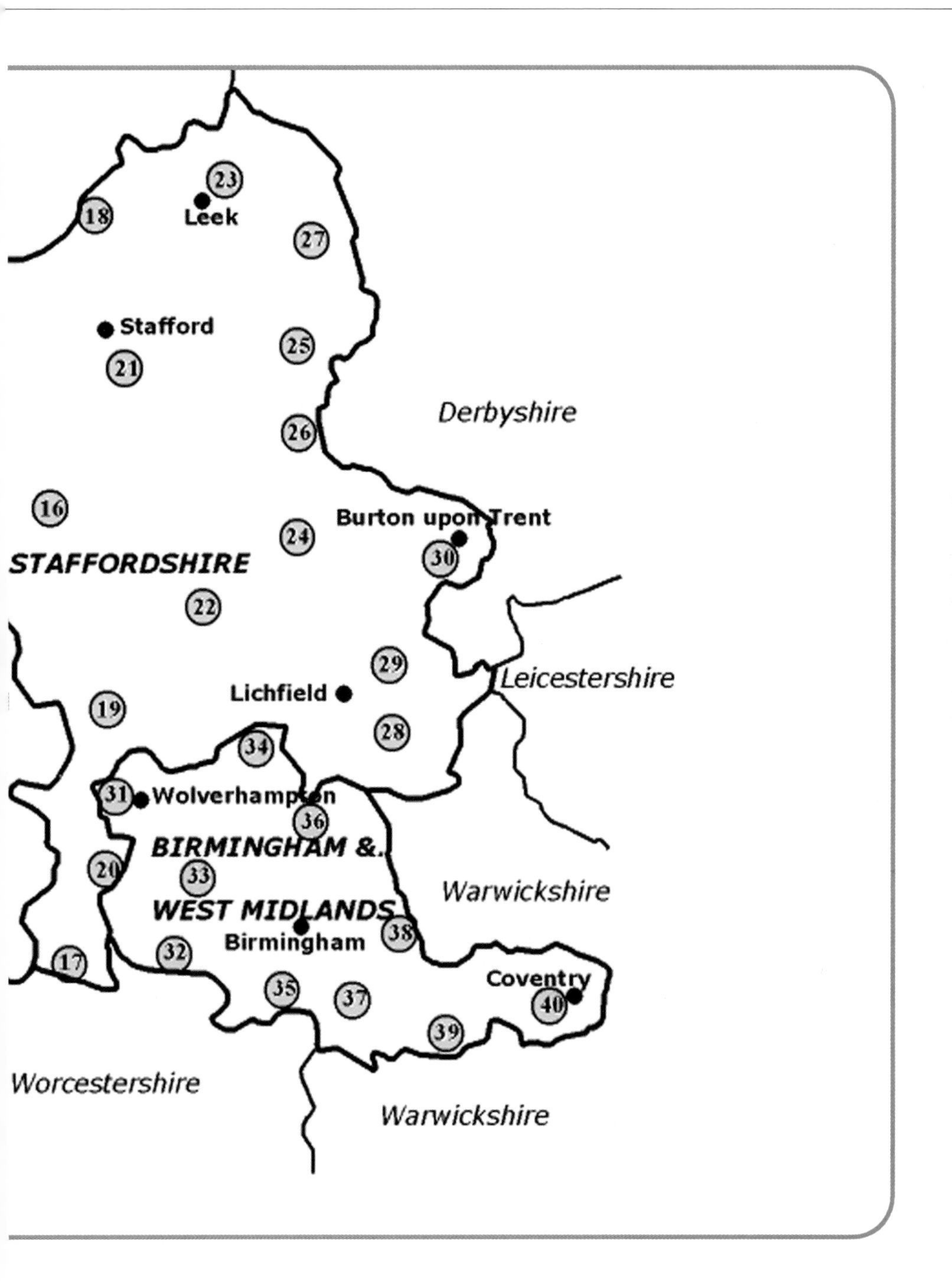
Leek
Stafford
Derbyshire
Burton upon Trent
STAFFORDSHIRE
Lichfield
Leicestershire
Wolverhampton
BIRMINGHAM &
WEST MIDLANDS
Birmingham
Warwickshire
Coventry
Worcestershire
Warwickshire
16
17
18
19
20
21
22
23
24
25
26
27
28
29
30
31
32
33
34
35
36
37
38
39
40

manufactured goods throughout the UK. An amazing network of waterways still operates throughout the whole area and provides a fascinating insight into our industrial past. James Brindley's Staffordshire and Worcestershire Canal transported coal, ironware, glass, pottery and textiles; his Trent and Mersey Canal transported the china clay needed by Josiah Wedgwood; and his Coventry Canal carried coal. Thomas Telford's Shropshire Union Canal transported freight from the West Country to Ellesmere Port. Sadly, the advent of railways and motor transport forced the canals into redundancy. No longer used to carry industrial loads, they today offer a major leisure attraction, providing a fascinating glimpse into history and easy walking access to the many picturesque villages in the area.

Several attractive rivers add a further dimension to a number of the walks in this book. The Trent, the Manifold and the Churnett carve their way through Staffordshire, while the Severn passes through Bridgnorth and Shrewsbury in Shropshire. Tittesworth Reservoir and Ellesmere Lakes, while noted for their superb scenery, provide a haven for wildlife. Wenlock Edge, the Long Mynd, the Stiperstones, the Wrekin and the Clee Hills in Shropshire and The Roaches and Kinver Edge in Staffordshire make for magnificent hill walks and panoramic views.

The walks vary in length from 3 miles to 8 miles. The surfaces underfoot are generally good. In dry weather normal outdoor footwear is likely to be adequate for the shorter walks. In wet weather or during the winter months, some stretches of footpath may require stout, waterproof boots or shoes, and then it is also advisable to be prepared with wet weather clothing.

With each walk there is a sketch map of the route, which should prove adequate to guide you. Nevertheless, Ordnance Survey Explorer maps to the scale of 1:25,000 are recommended, because they are specially designed for ramblers and provide more detailed information.

Where the starting point for the walk is the pub, this usually means that you can leave your car in their car park whilst doing the walk so long as you intend to call in for some refreshment. However, it is only courteous to seek permission from the landlord before setting out.

I wish you happy walking.

Roger Noyce

Bishop's Castle 1 Walk

The Boar's Head

This lovely walk starts from the middle of Bishop's Castle and takes you along a stretch of the Shropshire Way onto the Shropshire hills, designated an Area of Outstanding Natural Beauty. It follows part of an ancient drovers' road across the hilltops – tracks that have been in use since prehistoric times. The scenery is inspiring as you walk along the valley and then ascend over farm fields before descending into Bishop's Castle, once an important coaching town on the route from London to Montgomery. The town hall is a handsome brick building dating from 1765, and to the side of this is one of the older houses of Bishop's Castle, called the House on Crutches.

***Distance:** 4½ miles*

OS Explorer 216
GR 323887

An undulating walk through typical Shropshire countryside

Starting point: The car park between High Street and Station Road in Bishop's Castle.

How to get there: Bishop's Castle is 19 miles north-west of Ludlow. Leave Ludlow on the A49. In 9 miles, turn left onto the A489 and then, as you approach the town, turn left into Union Street to find the car park.

The **Boar's Head** is one of the earliest surviving buildings in Bishop's Castle, displaying exposed beams, large inglenooks and a recently discovered priest's hole. First licensed in 1642 during the Civil War, it remained unscathed when the Royalists burned the town in 1645. Later it became an important staging post for coaches. Food on offer ranges from snacks like soup and filled rolls through to cottage pie, lasagne and 'sizzling' steaks.

***Opening times** are from 11.30 am to 2.30 pm (3 pm on Saturday) and from 6.30 pm to 11 pm, from Monday to Saturday, and all day from 12 noon to 10.30 pm on Sunday. Food is available between noon and 2 pm and from 6.30 pm to 9.30 pm each day.*

***Telephone:** 01588 638521.*

The Walk

❶ From the car park stroll through to the High Street and head left, passing the Boar's Head hotel as you descend Church Street towards St John's church. At the end of the road turn right and then go left into Field Lane. Follow this section of the Shropshire Way in a south-westerly direction, passing a cottage and continuing over a stile by a farm gate. Walk along the clear hedged farm path for the next 500 yards, going over a series of stiles and through farm gates. (To your left ahead you will see the village of Colebatch, with the Long Mynd in the background.) Go over a final stile to descend towards a farm gate.

❷ Do not go through the gate, but turn right, walking to the right of the field hedge as you continue along the Shropshire Way, now in a north-westerly direction along the bottom of an attractive valley. Walk along this clear route for the next 500 yards, going over a couple of field stiles. As you progress, you will see Lower Woodbatch Farm to your right. A couple of stiles lead over a lane, and then you continue in the same north-westerly

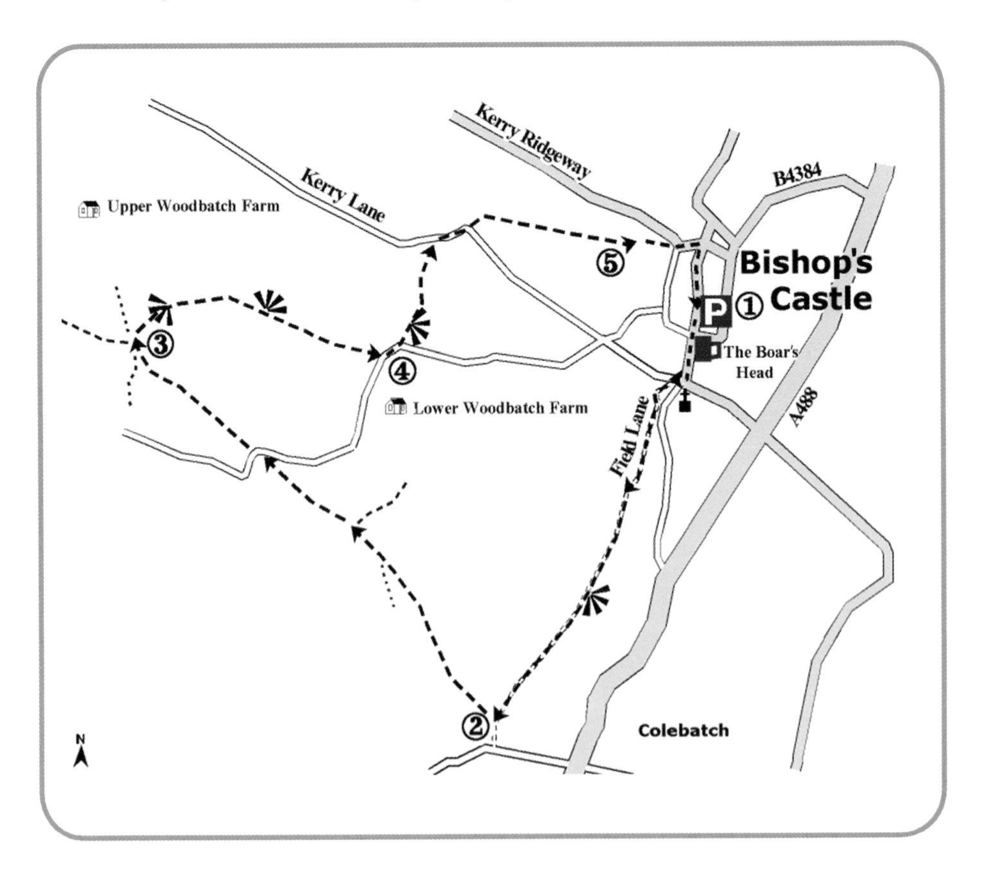

direction. Now Upper Woodbatch Farm is visible on the hill ahead; soon you reach a junction of footpaths.

The view from the Shropshire Way

3 Go over the stile to the right, and walk along the footpath that arcs right past a small duck pond. The route then arcs left, climbing beside the field fence to the top of the hill. (Do pause from time to time to enjoy the view of the valley behind you.) A stile leads into a large cultivated field, and you then walk near its right-hand hedge. (As you approach the end of the field, there is a good view of the Long Mynd to your right.) Go over the stile at the field end, and then descend gently to the right, onto a farm track that leads down to a lane.

4 Head left up the lane for about 50 yards; then turn left, going over stiles and passing through a corner copse. You will arrive in pastureland, where another good view of the Long Mynd will catch the eye. You are now walking in a more northerly direction as you cross several fields and stiles, eventually arriving on Kerry Lane. Head right along this quiet lane for some 35 yards, and then bear left over a stile onto a footpath that leads towards the village of Bishop's Castle.

5 Follow the waymarker signs. Eventually, you go over a stile into a residential area and stroll through to an estate road. Now bear left, and then turn right onto a footpath that takes you to the left of a high garden wall. At the end of this you will arrive in Union Street. Turn left and then right and you will pass by the House on Crutches as you bear right into the High Street. Stroll down the High Street and go left up an alleyway to return to the car park.

Date walk completed:

....

Places of Interest

Roundton Hill Nature Reserve, a wildlife trust reserve and Site of Special Scientific Interest that can be found off the A489, west of Bishop's Castle. Telephone: 01743 241691.

Walcot Hall Arboretum, 3½ miles west of Bishop's Castle, this 30-acre garden was developed by the son of Lord Clive of India. Telephone: 01588 680570.

Walk 2

Oswestry

The Eagles Inn

A lovely walk in the Shropshire countryside in the area of Offa's Dyke, along the border with Wales. You can soak up the atmosphere of times past as you stroll along part of the famous ancient earthworks, near the town of Oswestry. The Iron Age hill fort at Old Oswestry is chronicled in the folklore of King Arthur as the birthplace of Queen Guinevere. There are delightful views to enjoy on this circuit.

Distance: *6 miles*

OS Explorer 240
GR 258305

A hilly walk along comfortable footpaths, ending with an ascent of part of Offa's Dyke

Starting point: The car park and picnic area near Racecourse Common by the B4580 road, north-west of Oswestry.

How to get there: Oswestry is some 18 miles north-west of Shrewsbury. The A5 leads to the town.

The **Eagles Inn** will be found in Bailey Head, and there is safe parking in front of the pub. It is a delightful place, offering a warm welcome and good food, ideal for a snack prior to exploring the town. Tasty sandwiches are available or perhaps a sizzling tender steak may be your preference. It is also very pleasant to sit outside the inn, watching the world go by as you relax after your walk.

Opening times *are from 12 noon to 11 pm during the week, and from 12 noon to 10.30 pm on Sunday. Food is available between 11 am and 3 pm and 5pm and 10.30 pm every day.*

Telephone: *01691 661154.*

The Walk

1 From the car park, head left along the wide grass track by the roadside, going generally northwards to the B4580. Cross over the B-road and go ahead up the grass track on the right of the main road. In about 250 yards, the track bends right, away from the road, becoming the common land of Old Oswestry racecourse. Walk along the former racetrack as it arcs right, passing by a viewing bench, where you can enjoy an impressive view of the hills of the Long Mynd. About 75 yards after passing the bench, turn left up a footpath. This leads through bushes and rowan trees to emerge at a stile. Go over this and bear left to reach a lane and a cottage. Head left up the lane, and, in about 25 yards, turn right and go over a stile into the trees of Glopa Wood. After about 100 yards, you emerge into the open once again, via another stile, and should now aim for a mid-field stile. After crossing this stile, aim for the far left-hand corner of the next field. Go over the stile onto a driveway and head right, down the tarmac road, for about 300 yards; the tarmac road soon becomes a white road.

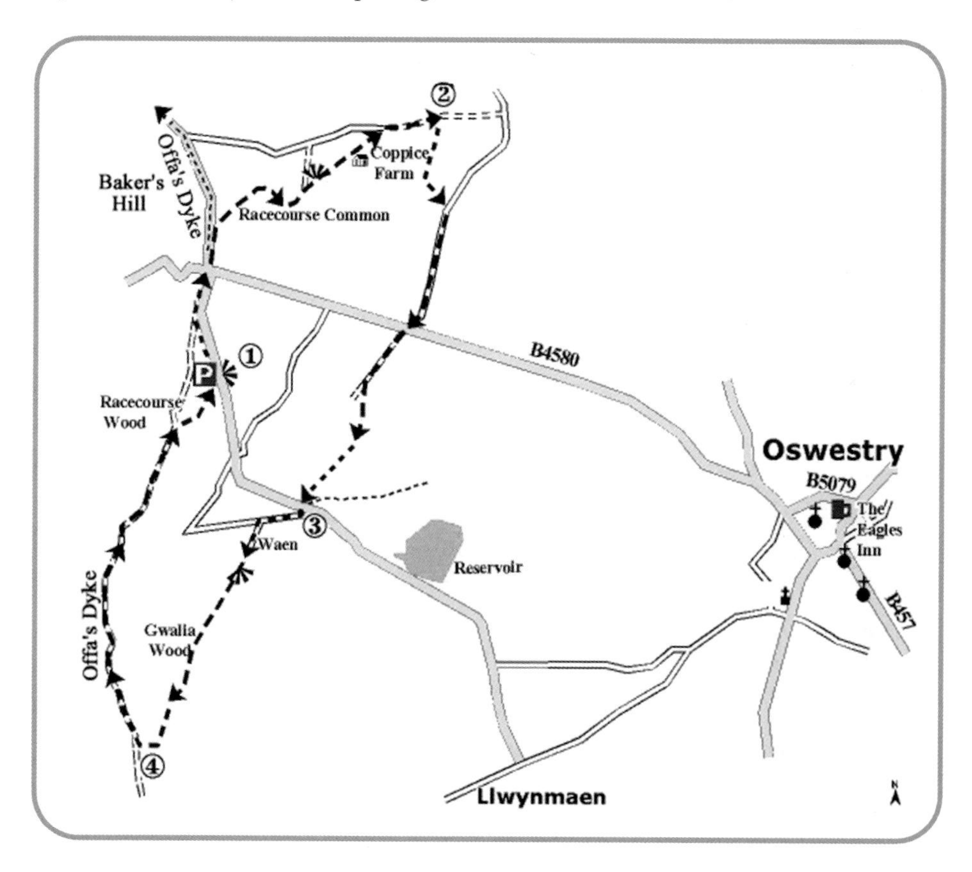

2 Turn right through a farm gate into pastureland; then walk along the left edge of the field, passing woodland to reach a second stile into a further stretch of woodland. The path descends into the trees by a pheasant-nesting area, and then bends left, becoming a wide woodland track to the road. Turn right along the road; after about half a mile of easy walking, you will arrive at the B4580. Cross over the road with care and enter the driveway (a dead-end road) opposite. After passing through a farm gate, it becomes a wide track, which you follow for the next 350 yards, looking out for a farm gate on the left. Go through the gate and an opening to the left of the small area of woodland in the far left corner of the field. Then head right, along the right edge of the field. After going over a fence by the next area of woodland, cross the next field and go through the farm gate onto the road.

The Offa's Dyke path

3 Turn right and then go left down a road (almost opposite). In 50 yards the road bends right. In a further 250 yards, turn left up the driveway to a private house called Waen. Where the driveway bends left, go ahead over a stile into an enclosed area by the hedge. A second stile takes you into pastureland. Follow the left-hand edge of the next field until you reach another stile, which you climb over. Cross the next field to a stile into Gwalia Wood. (In wet weather this can be rather muddy.) Go through the wood, leaving via a stile by a small pond into pastureland. Then continue across the next field to a stile by a farm gate; cross the stile and go right. Climb over a further stile by the woodland ahead of you. Walk along the signed footpath for the next 300 yards. Although it may be indistinct, there are waymarkers, and eventually you will reach a track coming in from the left.

4 Turn right and walk on to reach a junction of paths in about 300 yards. Turn right onto the historic Offa's Dyke Way National Trail as it climbs through the trees. Soon the trees thin out and you then walk by a wire fence with a clear view over the Shropshire Hills. Re-enter the woodland and soon reach a stile onto a wide track. Here, bear right, and then left, to continue on a footpath that will take you back to the parking area.

Place of Interest

Park Hall, Oswestry, a 130-acre farm, has a variety of attractions for the whole family: there are small animals and farm animals; opportunities to try hand-milking and pony grooming; quad bike rides, and a picnic area. Telephone: 01691 671123.

Date walk completed:

....

Stiperstones

The Stiperstones Inn

This panoramic walk takes you along the Stiperstone range of hills. The chain of jagged tors, designated an Area of Outstanding Natural Beauty, together with the Devil's Chair and Cranberry Rock, are Shropshire landmarks. Set amid heathland, this walker's paradise is ablaze with colour in the summer months, when the hills are also alive with skylarks, curlews, ravens and buzzards. The shorter route is designed to provide a taste of hill walking, while the longer version will suit the more seasoned rambler.

Distance: *5 miles or 7½ miles*

OS Explorer 216
GR363004

A hilly route, with generally good paths, which are rocky and more difficult underfoot near Manstone Rocks and Devil's Chair

Starting point: The Stiperstones Inn, Stiperstones.

How to get there: Stiperstones is 12 miles south-west of Shrewsbury. Follow the A488 and turn left ½ mile after Minsterley.

This award-winning pub, the **Stiperstones Inn**, is situated just below the Stiperstone hills. It offers a warm welcome to walkers and also has accommodation available. Delicious food at reasonable cost is served each day. Who could resist the delicious baked whinberry pie?

Opening times *are from 11 am to 11 pm every day and food is available all day long.*

Telephone: *01743 791327.*

The Walk

❶ From the Stiperstones Inn go past the telephone box; then turn right through Mytton Vale bus depot. Bear right over a stile and continue left along a hillside footpath going generally northwards. Initially, this is like a balcony walk, with glorious open views to your left, and then it edges round Oak Hill, with a barbed wire fence to your left. The green path tends to twist, turn and undulate until you go through a hand gate and walk in front of a white cottage. The route arcs left and then right to join a stone track, which you walk down to reach the road, passing Crow's Nest Farm.

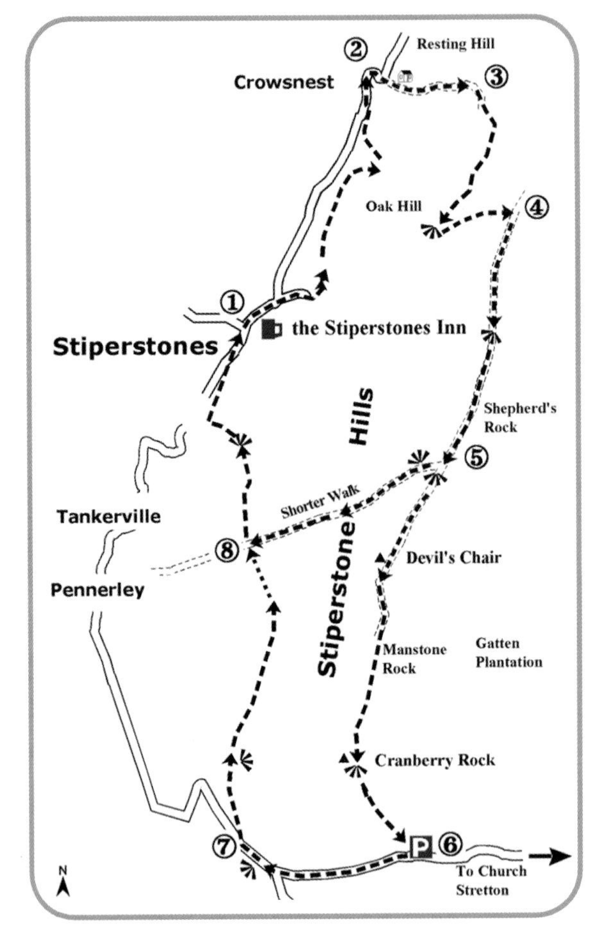

❷ Head right along the valley road, bearing right to go through the hamlet of Crowsnest. (Resting Hill is to your left and Oak Hill high to your right.)

❸ The lane bends right and you start to ascend along a footpath, now in a southerly direction. (In about 650 yards you reach the top of the valley and can enjoy some exhilarating views; the village of Stiperstones nestles to the right below.) When you reach a clear track, go sharp left, and beside a wall/fence climb to the main track on the top of Stiperstones Hill.

❹ Head right along this wide, mainly green track and climb the heather-clad ridge. (As you progress, Devil's Chair becomes ever more prominent ahead and there is a panoramic view to enjoy.) After almost a mile, you meet a track descending to the right.

❺ Here you have the option of taking the short walk or the longer walk.

To complete the **short walk**, turn right and descend on a good track to rejoin the route at point 8 on the map.

For the **longer walk**, continue

along the ridge track to Devil's Chair. It becomes rocky, but your effort will be rewarded by panoramic views.

Legend says that the Devil attempted to fill the valley between the Stiperstones and the Long Mynd with boulders. The rocky outcrops are said to have formed when he rose from his chair and his apron strings broke, dropping the rocks.

Continue along the rocky ridge track past Manstone Rock – the highest point on the Stiperstones, at 536m – and Cranberry Rock, with yet more wonderful views. The track now arcs gently left and becomes a green track as it descends to a stile and a car park.

6 From the car park go down to the road and turn right; at the road junction, keep right.

7 In about 220 yards (after passing the Shropshire Way Path signs), go right over a stile onto a waymarked path. Head right over a stile and cross a couple of fields along a clear green track set to the right of a fence/low stone wall, now going generally north-east. (The three rock formations you passed on the ridge track are now prominent on the skyline to your right.) When you reach a path junction, go left, keeping the wall to your left. In about 325 yards, go left through a field gate and diagonally cross pastureland to reach and go over a stile onto a main track.

8 If completing the **short walk**, turn right onto a fern-lined path.

If completing the **longer walk,** cross the main track to go down the fern-lined path, which heads north initially, and then arcs left, descending sharply to a stile into pastureland. Go over the stile, pausing to enjoy the view ahead of Stiperstone village, with the Welsh mountains beyond. Go down the field, bearing right at the bottom. Follow the clear footpath by the field hedge. On approaching the first house in the village, go over a stile and go left to reach the road. Head right along the quiet road through the village, passing by a school, to reach the Stiperstones Inn.

On the Stiperstone Hills

Place of Interest

Snailbeach Industrial Heritage Site is 5 miles north. Snailbeach village used to be one of the most important lead mines in Britain but is now a place of picturesque industrial ruins surrounded by green and blossom. Telephone: Shropshire County Council for further details: 01691 624448 or email: enquiries@shropshireroots.org.uk.

Date walk completed:

....

Walk 4 Ruyton XI Towns

The Talbot Inn

Ruyton XI Towns, the only place in the world with Roman numerals in its name, is a historic village situated by the river Perry. Many of its older buildings are constructed of the red sandstone which underlies the area. The Domesday Book records Ruyton, then spelled Ruitone, as a small manor of one and a half hides of land, containing five fisheries, held by the knight Odo under Earl Roger and formerly held by a Saxon nobleman, Leofnoth, under the Welsh prince Gwrgeneu ab Ednowain ab Ithel. A short road walk leads from the village to Cliffe Hill and from there a superb stretch of heather-covered hills can be enjoyed on the way back to the village.

The **Talbot Inn** is a 16th-century coaching inn with a black and white exterior and a comfortable interior, full of character and low beams. It offers a good selection of beers and you will enjoy superb, freshly prepared home-cooked food, which you can select from the menu or from the specials board. It serves a traditional roast lunch on Sunday as well as a full menu. (My own particular weakness is the goat's cheese and red onion tart with tomato jam.)

Opening times *are from 7 pm to 11 pm, every evening and also at lunchtime on Saturday and Sunday. Food is available between 7 pm and 9 pm and from 12.30 pm to 2 pm on Saturday and Sunday. This is a popular place; so booking is advisable.*

Telephone: *01939 260663.*

Distance: *4 miles*

OS Explorer 240
GR 392221

A gentle walk along good tracks

Starting point: The Talbot Inn at Ruyton.

How to get there: Ruyton XI Towns is 9 miles south-east of Oswestry. Go south on the A5 for about 7 miles; then turn left and take the B4397 into the village.

The Walk

1 From the Talbot Inn go to the main road in Ruyton and turn right. In about 100 yards, turn right again, by the side of St John the Baptist primary school. At the end of the grassed area, bear left and then go right over a stile to walk along a path at the back of houses to a second stile. Continue to the left of the field hedge, passing to the left of a water board sub-station to reach and go over a stile onto a track. Turn right and then left along the good hedged track, walking in a generally south-westerly direction. After about half a mile, the track arcs right and you pass a cottage at Coton Side; the track then bends left into the woodland of Ruyton Moss. Soon it bends right and continues just inside the left-hand edge of the wood. (Parts of the track can be muddy in wet weather.) Continue beyond the end of the trees to a lane. Turn right and walk along the lane for about 100 yards, and then bear left towards a smallholding. At the corner, go over the stile to the right into

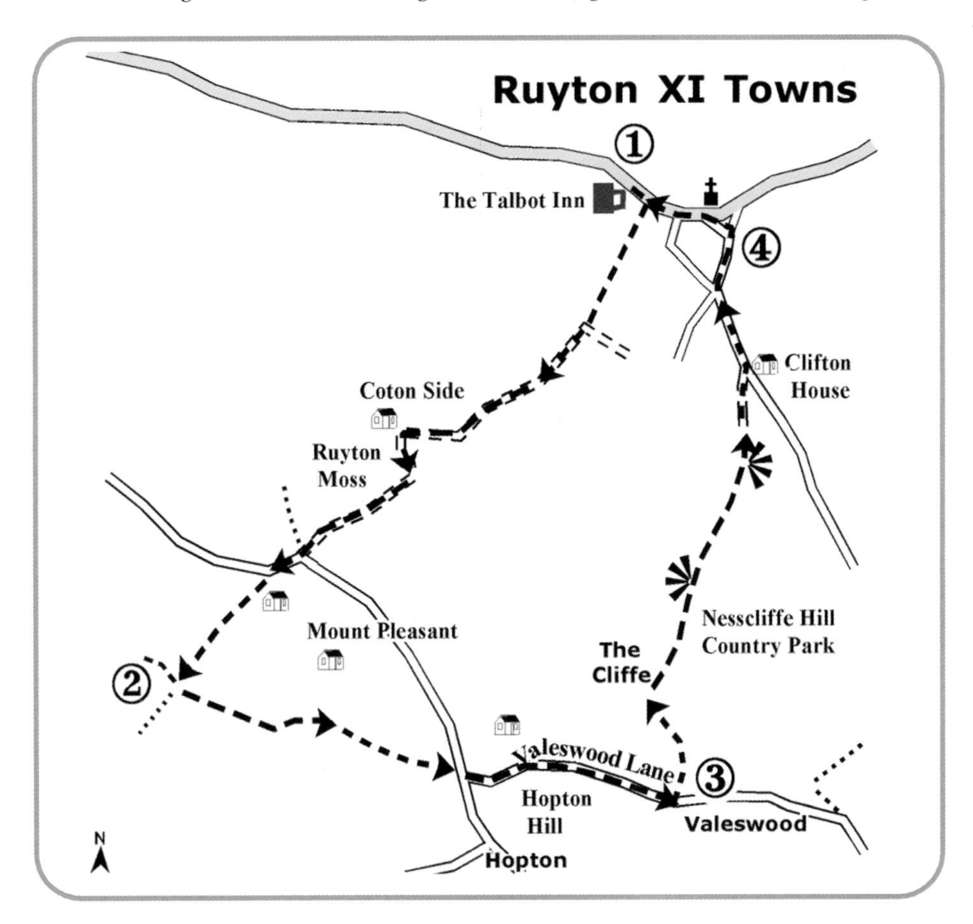

pastureland. Then walk through the field to the right of the smallholding. Continue over a field stile and walk along the left-hand edge of the next arable field to a gap in the hedge.

Looking towards the Cliffe

2 Pass through this gap and turn sharp left. (There is a waymarker half hidden in the hedge.) Now walk to the right of the field hedge (originally the footpath was to its left) over three fields to reach a farm gate. Pass through the farm gate and continue ahead, now to the left of the field hedge, to a stile in the hedge, with Mount Pleasant to your left. Continue over the next two fields to emerge on the road by a cottage. Turn right, and then go left up Valeswood Lane. In about 800 yards you will pass a track going off to your right into the trees on Hopton Hill and will then arrive at a junction (there are more tracks going off to the right).

3 Turn left past a large cottage and ascend the hill behind it. Follow the sandy path, though there are areas of rock to negotiate as you climb. At the top of The Cliffe you arrive by a Nesscliffe Hill Country Park board. Go down the path to the right of the reservoir fence. (The Wrekin can be seen on the horizon to your right.) Follow the clear wide heather-lined track over the hill. After about half a mile, you reach a building, with a track coming in from the right. Turn left and stroll down to a junction of stone tracks near to a noticeboard. Head down the main track to the road by Clifton House. Turn left and walk down the quiet road into the village of Ruyton.

4 Just after passing Birch Grove, turn left and go down Gooseberry Lane. Soon you will reach the main road in the village. Turn left to return to the Talbot Inn.

Place of Interest

Whittington Castle, 8 miles north-west, dates from the 12th century. Little remains intact apart from the impressive crenellated gatehouse towers of red sandstone, and the old moat. More details can be found at www.shropshiretourism.info/castles/whittington or telephone Oswestry Tourist Information Centre: 01691 662753.

Date walk completed:

....

Ellesmere Lakes

The Red Lion

This easy attractive walk offers the opportunity to visit Shropshire's own lake district and to wander round a beautiful historic town. Nestling between The Mere and the Shropshire Union canal, the small market town of Ellesmere is a picture of floral colour during the summer months, and has won the Britain in Bloom competition many times. From Colemere Country Park you walk along the canal towpath to the wharf in Ellesmere. On the way you go through one of the earliest tunnels to carry a towpath and pass Blake Mere, a lake left by glaciers some 12,000 years ago, and limekilns that once served the area. After going through the town, you enter into delightful countryside before completing the walk along a final stretch of towpath and through woodland.

Distance: 6 miles

OS Explorers 240 and 241
GR 436329

An easy walk along canal towpaths and generally good footpaths and farm tracks

Starting point: Colemere Country Park car park.

How to get there: Ellesmere is 8 miles north-east of Oswestry, off the A495 road.

The **Red Lion** is a 16th-century coaching inn, set next to St Mary's church. Here you can look forward to a warm welcome, cask ales, a wide selection of wines and an excellent meal of home-made quality food. Choose from sandwiches, salads, snacks, baked potatoes, grills, starters, fish dishes, traditional pub fare, and dishes from a specials board.

Opening times *are all day every day of the week. Food is served between noon and 8.30 pm.*

Telephone: *01691 622632.*
Website: *www.ellesmere.info/redlion*

The Walk

❶ From the car park, go towards the lake and head left around the side of the fence to the sailing club area. Go round the end of the fencing and bear right onto a footpath, which you follow past a black and white boathouse. Then continue along the woodland footpath to the south of the lake. At the end of the lake, bear right down a lane, passing a pretty thatched cottage, and crossing over the canal bridge. Now turn left, descend to the towpath of the Llangollen canal, and head right towards Ellesmere town. This is easy walking on a good level towpath, and you are likely to see a number of narrowboats making their way along Thomas Telford's contour canal. After about 2 miles, you will arrive by Blackwater Meadow Marina, where numerous narrowboats are moored.

❷ In a further 250 yards you will reach Ellesmere Wharf, which is an attractive dead-end stretch of the canal. Cross over the footbridge and walk on the towpath into the town (or perhaps rest on one of the wharf-side benches and take in the sleepy atmosphere of the canal). From the end of the canal, enter Ellesmere by walking up Wharf Road to the town centre. Turn right into Scotland Street, and then bear right through the town centre car park to reach Church Road. Turn right here, and you will find the Red

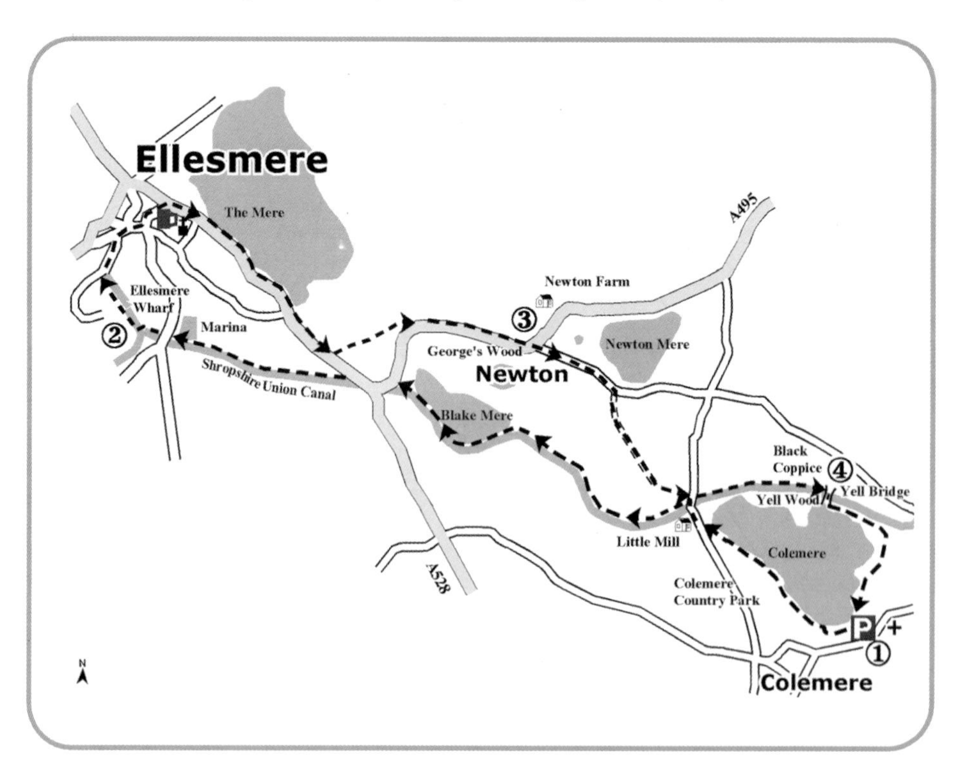

Lion public house on the right. Cross over the road with care and continue along the pavement, passing by St Mary's church, to arrive near the visitor centre and the tourist information office. To the left is a fine view of The Mere (the largest of the Ellesmere lakes). Continue along the grass verge on the left-hand edge of the road for about 600 yards, and then go left over a stile to follow a clear footpath up the bank. In about 300 yards, you will see the road below, but continue inside the fence until you reach a second stile onto the road (just round the bend in the road). Cross the stile onto the road, and now walk along the side of the road with very great care, as it is fairly narrow and there is no pavement or grass verge.

The Llangollen canal

3 After about half a mile, cross the road with care, and walk along the quiet lane opposite, past houses in the tiny village of Newton. After about 400 yards, you will see Newton Mere to your left. As you continue, look out for a track going off to the right; this will be found where the lane draws close to the mere. Do not go down the hedged track but take the farm track set to its left. This is a lovely grass track that arcs gently left. Soon you will reach a large oak tree with a clear waymarker attached to it. Shortly after it, the track bends left, and you should now look out for a footpath bearing off to the right. Walk along this footpath, which arcs right, and enter the trees, descending to the canal bridge near to Little Mill. Take the towpath to the left of the canal and follow it, enjoying the easy walk, with Colesmere visible through the trees to your right. In about half a mile you will reach Yell Bridge.

4 Go beneath the bridge and turn left; then cross the bridge over the canal into Yell Wood, keeping to the clear wide footpath through the trees. Initially, the path goes generally east; then it arcs right through the trees to reach a kissing gate onto pastureland near to Colesmere Country Park, with a good view of the mere to your right. Walk on the grass path to a kissing gate, and return to the car park.

Place of Interest

Chirk Castle (National Trust), 7 miles north, is a magnificent 14th-century fortress of the Welsh Marches. Telephone: 01691 777701.

Date walk completed:

....

Craven Arms

The Stokesay Castle Hotel

Starting in Craven Arms, this route follows good footpaths into attractive countryside and visits impressive 13th-century Stokesay Castle before returning along the side of the River Onny. Craven Arms grew up as an important railway junction. It takes its name from the Craven Arms inn, which was probably built in the early 1800s, having taken its name from the earls of Craven, who were lords of the nearby manor of Stokesay in the early 17th century. Today, the town is a typical small agricultural community; it has a large abattoir, a food processing plant and a thriving livestock market. There are some pleasant Edwardian and late Victorian shops to explore.

Distance: *3½ miles*

OS Explorer 217
GR 433828

An easy walk

Starting point: The public car park in Craven Arms

How to get there: Craven Arms is situated on the A49 road, about 8 miles north-west of Ludlow.

The **Stokesay Castle Hotel**, dating back to the 19th century, can be found in School Road, Craven Arms. The food, which ranges from sandwiches, jacket potatoes, baguettes and flatbreads to bar meals and à la carte can be enjoyed in the beamed lounge, the wood-panelled Portcullis restaurant or the large garden area.

Opening times *are from 11 am to 11 pm, Monday to Saturday, and from noon to 10.30 am on Sunday. Food is served every day between 12.30 pm and 3 pm and from 7 pm to 9 pm.*

Telephone: *01588 672304.*

The Walk

❶ From the car park, walk along the A49 Ludlow road for 225 yards, passing the Craven Arms Hotel and crossing the B4368 Clun road. Soon after passing the fire station and an antiques showroom, go right into Dodd's Lane.

The lane will take you beneath a railway bridge, and you will soon be walking on a clear track. After crossing a stile, bear left onto a footpath that hugs the left-hand hedge as you progress over four fields, going over several stiles and through a gate. (To your right, you will find there is a lovely view that embraces Sallow Coppice.) The path arcs generally left, and in the middle of the next field you will meet a clear path coming from the right. Turn left and walk on this path, aiming for a corner stile near an attractive white cottage at Clapping Wicket.

❷ Now bear left onto a forest track that leads you along the edge of Stoke Wood. This is a delightful green track and you can expect to enjoy a display of colourful wild flowers in summer. After walking along the track for some 650 yards, turn left over a stile into pastureland. (Here there is a particularly good view of Stokesay Castle, set against a backdrop of the Shropshire hills.) As you go down the clear path over several fields and stiles

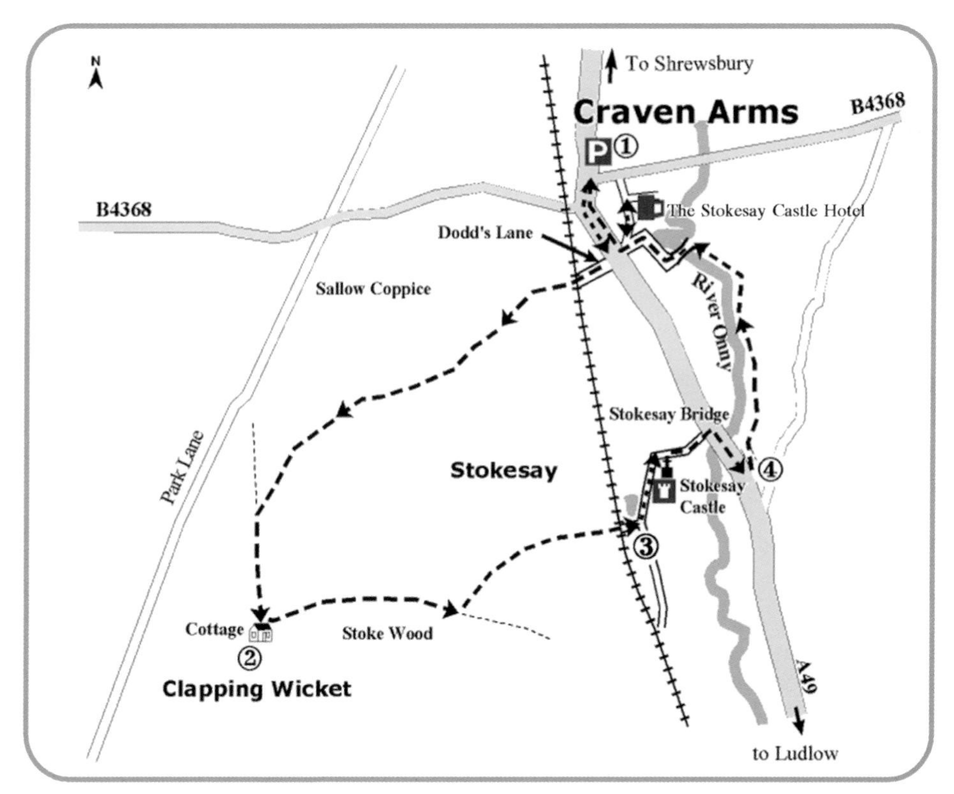

and approach the mainline railway, the castle gets ever closer. Take great care crossing the railway track, and then follow the farm lane to the left before going through a gate onto Castle Lane.

The romantic 13th-century Stokesay Castle

3 Now turn left and walk past the impressive castle.

Entrance can be made through the churchyard of the church of St John the Baptist. The church was built as a chapel to the castle, in about 1150. This interesting building has a lovely 17th-century gallery, used by musicians and choristers until about 1855, and below it there are five primitive pews.

Continue along the lane past the car park until you reach the A49. Turn right to cross the River Onny by Stokesay bridge, and then cross with care over the busy road.

4 In 120 yards, turn left and go down a stretch of disused road. At its end, turn right and descend steps that lead to the riverside path back to Craven Arms. After a couple of stiles, the path arcs left, first across a footbridge and then across a white metal footbridge over the River Onny. You will enter the town along Newton Road. Turn right and walk on the pavement, passing attractive old half-timbered buildings (the Old Rectory is particularly nice). At the end of Newton Road, turn left into School Road (if you are ready for refreshment, the Stokesay Castle Hotel is at the end of this road). Soon you will reach the A49 Ludlow Road; here go right and walk on the pavement, back to your car.

Place of Interest

The **Shropshire Discovery Centre** in Craven Arms provides a fun day out discovering the secrets of the Shropshire Hills. There is a variety of exhibitions guiding the visitor through the geological history of the area and pointing out the key features of the Shropshire landscape. A unique simulated hot air balloon offers a flight from the Wrekin in the north to the Stiperstones in the south. Telephone: 01588 676000.

Date walk completed:

....

Carding Mill Valley

The Yew Tree, All Stretton

Any walk along the Long Mynd is a treat, especially in good weather. The Long Mynd is a long ridge without any particular peaks in the higher parts. It encloses a series of valleys, and these produce an impression of wilderness as you stroll along the rolling ridge top. After ascending Carding Mill Valley, this exhilarating walk takes you on to the famous ridge to experience a 'get away from it all feeling' amid a sea of heather and gorse and to enjoy the extensive views that embrace Caer Caradoc. A fairly gentle descent brings you into the village of All Stretton, where you can lunch at the Yew Tree.

Distance: *5½ miles*

OS Explorer 217
GR 441948

A superb hill walk with fine views

Starting point: The National Trust pay-and-display car park in Carding Mill Valley.

How to get there: Church Stretton is 13 miles south of Shrewsbury. Leave Shrewsbury on the A5112 and turn onto the A49. In about 12¾ miles, turn right onto the B4371 road and enter the town. Follow the National Trust signs to Carding Mill Valley.

The **Yew Tree** at All Stretton is situated in the centre of the village. It is on the Stretton Real Ale Trail and embodies the true tradition of old England, with good beer and good cheer. You will be intrigued by the collection of animal skulls that are displayed in this old pub. As well as bar snacks, the home-made food offers such mouth-watering morsels as deep-fried Camembert with redcurrant jelly, breast of chicken in a Stilton cheese sauce, and for pudding a crumble or scrumptious bread and butter pudding with orange marmalade.

Opening times *are from 12 noon until 2.30 pm (3 pm on Sunday) and from 7 pm until 11 pm daily. Food is served from 12 noon to 2 pm and from 7 pm to 11 pm.*

Telephone: *01694 722228.*

The Walk

1 From the National Trust car park, continue up Carding Mill Valley, passing the National Trust shop, tearooms and further parking area. Climb the stone footpath between Cow Ridge and Haddon Hill (467m), taking time to enjoy the very beautiful scenery (behind you, there is a particularly good view down the valley). At the junction of paths, turn right and continue along the bridleway path called Mott's Road, which climbs to the left, between Calf Ridge and Haddon Hill. After about a mile of steady ascent, you will reach the ridge of Long Mynd and a junction of paths

2 Turn right and proceed along the main track called The Port Way for about three-quarters of a mile. Initially, it is a wide stone way, later becoming a tarmac road, and you cross over a ford. At the cattle grid, bear right and descend for about 400 yards until you meet a track coming in from the right; continue your descent along this track, going over Cross Dyke. As the track arcs right, you descend with Jonathan's Rock to your right; it

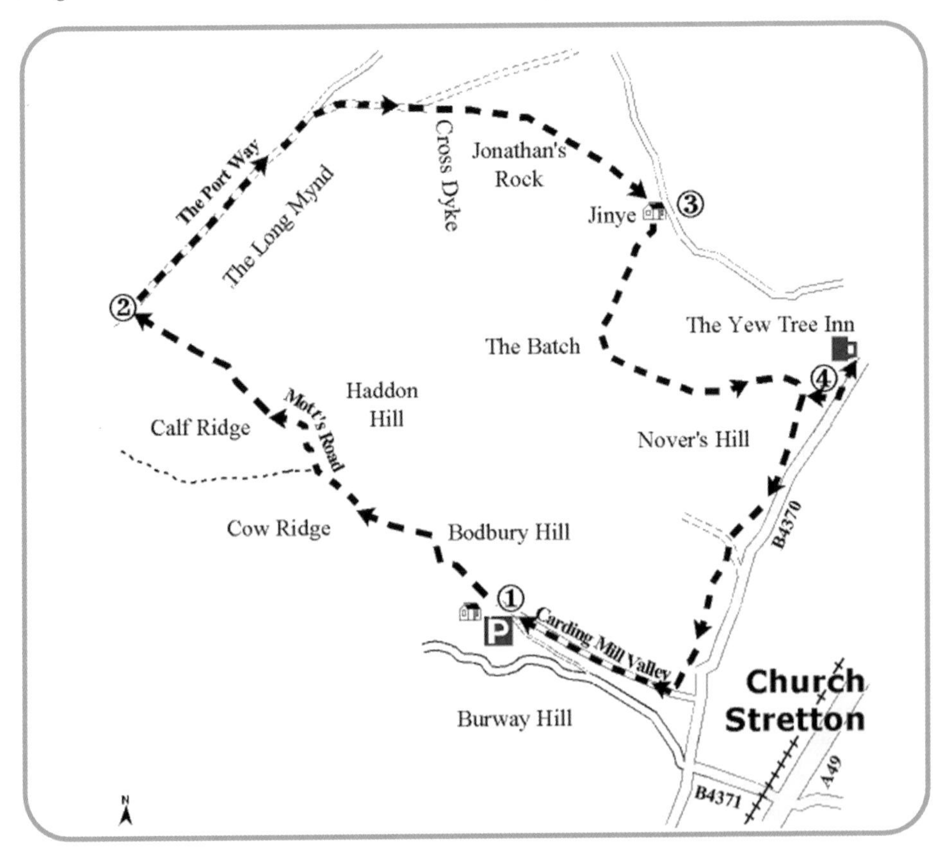

then becomes a footpath, passing to the back of Plush House. Bear right here onto a permissive footpath and continue to the left of a spring, with a building, Jinye, to your left by the side of a lane.

3 Continue along the footpath, following the sign that directs you left down the valley, with Haddon Hill initially appearing to be ahead of you. The path bends left on a hill ledge, which can involve a small scramble. Continue your descent, walking to the left of a wire fence, with a cottage to the right in the valley below. At the drive to the cottage, turn left to continue your descent. You pass by a small pool with a building (in the field to the right), after which the track becomes a tarmac lane. Cross the small bridge by a ford on the lane, which arcs left, and to the left ahead you will see some cottages. Walk down to the entrance to the cottages, cross over the stream, and then climb up the well-defined path, going right towards a stile.

4 Go over the stile and bear right, towards a half-timbered house. Walk to the left of this to get to the main road in All Stretton and the Yew Tree. After refreshment retrace your steps to the half-timbered dwelling, and bear left over a stile onto a footpath that goes along the back of residential houses on the B4370 road. Above the houses, there is a delightful view towards Caradoc, Helmett and Raglett hills as you negotiate a couple of kissing gates. Immediately after the second gate, the path bears right, away from the B4370. There is a bench, from which you can enjoy another view of Caradoc Hill. As you continue, you descend to a kissing gate to the lane to Cwmdale. Cross over this lane and go

Carding Hill Valley

through the gate opposite onto a pleasant path through trees to arrive on a residential road called Madeira Walk. Continue along this road of well-maintained black and white half-timbered houses. Soon you will reach the road to Carding Mill Valley, where you turn right and walk up the quiet road to return to the National Trust car park.

Place of Interest

Stokesay Castle (English Heritage), built in the 13th century, is one of the finest fortified manor houses in England. Its earliest occupants were the de Sayes, who fortified the building to keep out Welsh marauders. The right tower is surmounted by a 16th-century half-timbered storey, and there is a great gabled banqueting hall with tall gothic windows. The eye-catching black and white Elizabethan gatehouse offers a fine photo opportunity. Telephone: 01588 672544.

Date walk completed:

....

Walk 8 Uffington

The Corbet Arms

This pleasant walk in typical Shropshire countryside includes part of the Shropshire Way. Public footpaths take you past an impressive castle-like building on the old Sundorne estate and onto farmland. The estate was established by John Corbett, a local MP, in the late 1700s. The so-called castle started as a house, but was transformed by him to look like a vast castle. The return route, over lovely farmland, passes the ruins of Haughmond Abbey, which was built in the 12th century. The remains of the old abbey contain an exhibition to commemorate 600 years since the Battle of Shrewsbury.

Distance: *6½ miles*

OS Explorer 241
GR 542150

An easy walk along mainly good footpaths and farm tracks

Starting point: Roden Lane car park

How to get there: Uffington is 4½ miles east of Shrewsbury. Leave Shrewsbury on the B5062 road and cross over the A49. In about a mile, turn right down the signed local road to reach the village.

The **Corbet Arms**, Uffington, is well positioned with excellent views. It has a particularly nice garden and is a pleasure to visit. You are assured of a warm welcome, and 'lite bites' and vegetarian dishes are offered, plus a good range of wholesome meals, such as salmon and dill lasagne and home-made chicken curry. Beers include Flowers Original beer.

Opening times *are from 12 noon to 3 pm and from 7 pm to 11 pm every day except Sunday, when the pub closes at 10.30 pm. Food is served between noon and 2 pm and from 7 pm to 9.30 pm in the evening (9 pm on Sunday).*

Telephone: *01743 70932.*

The Walk

1 From the car park, cross the B5062 road onto the tree-lined Shropshire Way opposite. In about three quarters of a mile, as you appear to near the end of the wood, turn left along a signed footpath inside the edge of the trees. In about 250 yards, turn right, and, on a footpath out of the trees, walk towards a country lane. Turn right and walk to a road junction on the edge of the village of Uffington; then head right along the main road to find the Corbet Arms, set back on the left.

2 Cross the road and continue up the short road opposite, signed 'Tower Farm 1-3'. In a few yards, go over a field stile to leave the village and rejoin the Shropshire Way. The path crosses a bridge; then you climb over a stile onto a footpath by electricity pylons. Turn left, and leave the Shropshire Way. In about 150 yards, you reach a junction of tracks and bear right. Then go left, following the waymarker direction towards the village sewage works. The footpath emerges into an open field. Follow the waymarker direction, aiming towards a stile onto the B5062 road. Cross the road, and go ahead along a fenced footpath to the right of the Burgess building, to reach a ditch in about 250 yards. Bear right, and then go left, descending over a footbridge. Head across the next field, aiming for a stile situated to the right of the castellated buildings of Sundorne Castle Farm. Turn left on the farm drive and pass below the former castle gateway. Then continue along the tarmac/concrete road, past a row of cottages and the main farm complex. After about

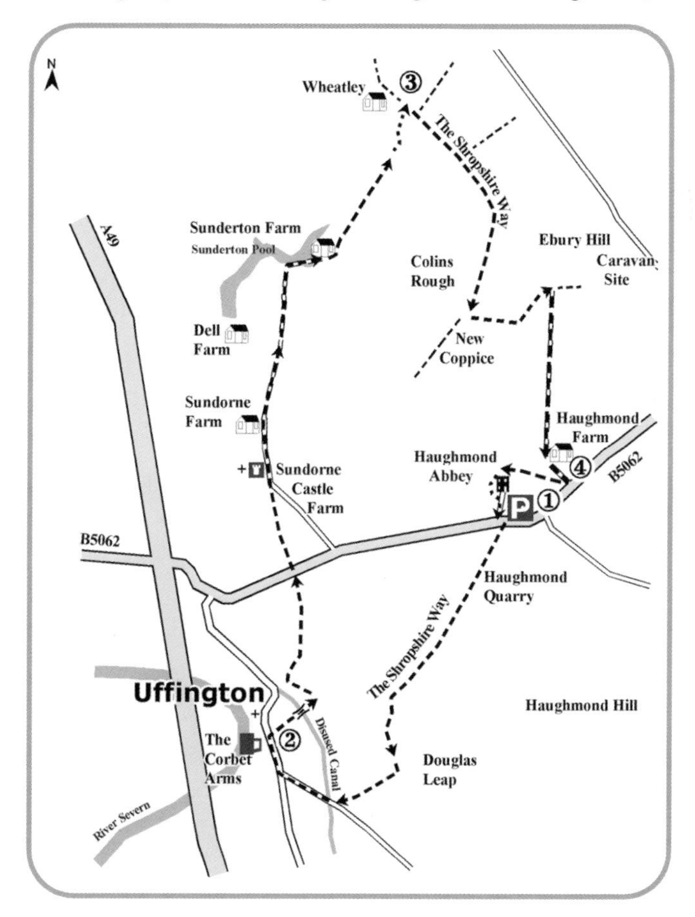

half a mile, you reach a large stretch of water (behind the bushes). Follow the driveway as it bends right, passing to the right of the farm complex of Sunderton; the track loops round the buildings. Then you head towards a farm gate near a lane. At the gate, bear left over a stile and keep to the left of the field hedge, away from the farm. After going over a rise in the pastureland, you drop down to a hand gate. Go through this and then soon go left again through a second hand gate to continue along the bridleway path, initially walking by the field's right-hand fence, but then aiming towards a marker post in front of the hedge ahead.

3 At the marker post, turn right and rejoin the Shropshire Way, walking to the field corner to go over the stile. After passing through a hand gate, continue to the left of the field hedge. The path arcs gently right and soon passes through another hand gate with Colin's Rough to your right. Cross the large field, following the Shropshire Way markers that lead you to a junction of footpaths between Colin's Rough and New Coppice. Turn left here, along the side of New Coppice, still on the Shropshire Way. At the field corner turn left, keeping to the left of the field fence on a footpath that arcs right towards a caravan site. About 100 yards from the caravan site, turn right and go down a wide hedged track going southwards.

Haughmond Abbey

(This track is used by the local farmer to move cattle and can be rather dirty or muddy in parts.) In about 400 yards, at Haughmond Farm, bear left just after reaching the main complex of buildings, and go along the main farmhouse driveway towards the B5062.

4 By the road turn sharp right and go over a corner stile. Then walk away from the road and the farm, in a north-westerly direction, to reach a high stile in the field hedge. Go over this and walk on the clearly defined footpath around Haughmond Abbey. Leave the abbey area along the driveway; then turn left at the B5062 to arrive back in the car park.

Date walk completed:

....

Places of Interest

Hawkstone Hall and Gardens, Marchamley, Shrewsbury, is a Georgian mansion set in superb parkland. Telephone: 01630 685242.

The Welshpool and Llanfair Railway is only half an hour away from Shrewsbury. Telephone: 01938 810441.

Ludlow

The Church Inn

It seems that wherever you are on this lovely walk Ludlow Castle is never far away. Perched on a cliff above the picturesque river Teme, the castle dominates the skyline and is very much part of Ludlow, a historic town of ordered elegance. The castle, church, medieval and Georgian buildings combine to make what John Betjeman described as 'The most perfect town in England', and it is well worth taking time to wander through its interesting streets, where so many half-timbered black and white buildings will catch your eye. The walk takes you across a bridge over the river Teme and then climbs up into imposing Mortimer Forest before descending to the river again to re-enter Ludlow over a second historic bridge.

Distance: *7 miles*

OS Explorer 203
GR 511746

A delightful walk on good footpaths and tracks

Starting point: Market Square, Ludlow

How to get there: Ludlow is a major Shropshire town, situated near to the A49 in the south-west corner of the county.

The **Church Inn** is over seven centuries old and over the years it has had many uses; it has served as the premises of a barber, a surgeon, a blacksmith, a saddler and a druggist. Originally the Cross Keys, the name was changed to the Church Inn in January 1979 to reflect the pub's situation as the nearest licensed house to St Laurence's church. Freshly cooked food at a reasonable price is the order of the day, and there is a wide selection on offer, from sandwiches to trout or steak. Accommodation is also available: nine rooms, all en suite.

Opening times *are from 11 am to 11 pm (10.30 pm on Sunday), and food is served between 12 noon and 2 pm and from 6.30 pm to 9 pm (8.30 pm on Sunday).*

Telephone: *01584 872174.*

The Walk

1 Leave Market Square by walking down College Street and stroll through this delightful town until you reach the B4361 road. Turn right and cross Ludford Bridge over the river Teme; then continue along the grass verge of the B4361 for nearly half a mile.

2 Now turn right and walk on the public footpath past a house called Mabbit's Barn. Walk along the driveway to the house, and then, where the driveway divides, bear left and continue ahead; the footpath becomes a green track by a farm gate. Walk through the pastureland, passing a farm road signed to Ludlow. About 100 yards beyond this road, the track divides and you continue ahead on the track set to the left of the hedge. The track becomes a path, and then you cross over a lane to arrive back at the B4361 on the edge of the village of Overton. Head right into Overton. In about 150 yards, at a bend in the B4361, bear right and follow the road to Mortimer Forest, passing the barrier and forestry notice (there is a stream to the right). In about 250 yards, you will reach a junction of tracks.

3 Bear right here, walking in a generally north-westerly direction along the Mary

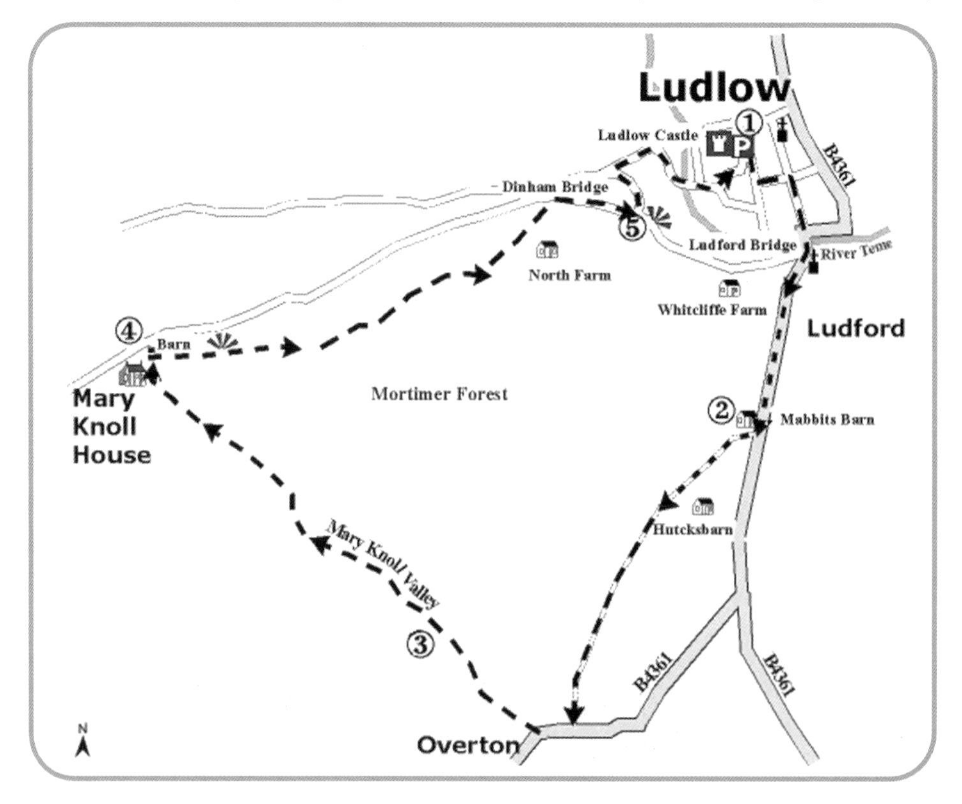

Knoll valley. At a meeting of forest tracks go right and walk by the cliff face. Then bear left onto a signed permissive path, following the line of the stream into a pine forest. Cross the stream to reach the forest road. Now bear right, and, in about 500 yards, turn right again to cross the stream; then bear left to continue along the path. (You should now be walking to the right of the stream in a north-westerly direction.) Eventually, the pine trees on the right are replaced by deciduous trees. Past these trees, as the main forest track arcs right, walk ahead along a footpath to the right of the stream. Further on, pass through a forest gate into pastureland, and then walk along a fenced footpath ascending out of the valley. After going through another forest gate you will soon reach Mary Knoll House.

❹ Turn right near the cottage, and pass the farm buildings to re-enter Mortimer Forest along a pleasant, hedged track. Bear left onto a hedged path and ascend gently onto open ground. The path soon becomes a track (adorned with wild flowers in spring), and there are fine views over the hill to the north. On reaching a junction of forest tracks, cross over and walk into the forest again on the path opposite, now following yellow marker posts until you reach a path inside the forest edge. Bear left and walk on this path, keeping by the edge of the trees, until you reach a quiet forest lane, where you turn right. Walk down the lane, reaching, in about 500 yards, the junction at Whitcliffe Road, near Whitcliffe Common (there is a view point here overlooking Ludlow Castle).

Ludlow - 'the most perfect town in England'

❺ Turn left and walk along the path on the common ground beside the road that arcs right, down to Dinham Bridge. Cross the bridge and go up the narrow lane, bearing gently left to arrive back in the Market Square.

Date walk completed:

....

Places of Interest

Ludlow Castle, an English castle on the Welsh Marches, served as an administrative centre for most of the 17th century, when Ludlow was effectively the capital of Wales, and its courts were busy with criminal, ecclesiastical and civil cases. Telephone: 01584 873355; e-mail: info@ludlowcastle.com.

St Laurence's church in Ludlow is well worth a visit. Originally Norman, it was rebuilt in 1199. You can climb the 200 steps to the top of its fine tower for a super view of the town. The church's exterior displays a memorial plaque to A. E. Houseman. Telephone: 01584 872073; website: www.stlaurences.org.uk.

Walk 10 Whitchurch

The Old Town Hall Vault

This gentle walk takes you through attractive gardens and along the towpath of the Shropshire Union canal, passing by Grindley Brook locks, where colourful narrowboats make their way through fascinating lock gates. The walk crosses over a golf course to return to Whitchurch (the home of JB Joyce & Co., the world famous makers of clocks), where a clock tour may appeal. Whitchurch's history dates back to Roman times, when it was known as Mediolanum. The church of St Alkmund stands on the site of an earlier Norman church, from which the town seems to have acquired its name, 'white church', probably denoting a church built of stone.

The **Old Town Hall Vault** in St Mary's Street, Whitchurch, is an intriguing pub set back from the High Street. It is the birthplace of the composer Edward German, whose works include operettas such as *Merrie England* and *Tom Jones*, and some original manuscripts and other memorabilia can be seen in the pub. This is considered the place to eat in Whitchurch. Its bar snacks can include steak and kidney pie and lasagne, and the pensioners' special is very popular.

***Opening times** are from 10 am (for coffee) until 2 pm and from 6 pm to 11 pm (10.30 pm on Sunday). Food is available between 12 noon and 2 pm every day, and also between 6 pm and 9 pm, Monday to Saturday. No food is served on Sunday evening.*

***Telephone:** 01948 662251.*

***Distance:** 5 miles*

OS Explorer 257
GR 540415

An easy walk along good footpaths and the canal towpath

Starting point: Castle Hill car park in Whitchurch.

How to get there: Whitchurch is on the A49 road, 20 miles north of Shrewsbury.

The Walk

1 From the car park go down into Victoria Park and walk through the park, bearing right to Sherrymill Hill. Cross the road and go ahead, following the waymarker of the Sandstone Trail. Go down the good stone footpath along the back of residential properties, eventually passing beneath a canal bridge to arrive by the side of the Shropshire feeder canal. Walk to the right of this up to a swing bridge, which you cross. Head right along the towpath of the main canal. After passing beneath Danson's bridge, the canal arcs gently north-eastwards, and, in about 500 yards, you arrive at Grindley Brook mooring area, followed by the Grindley Brook set of lock gates and the A41 road bridge. The canal bends left, and, after passing three more lock gates, you arrive at a canal bridge.

2 Cross the canal on the bridge or over the lock gate, and head right along a lane. After going beneath a bridge, bear left over a stile into pastureland. Follow the yellow waymarker signs for the South Cheshire Way (SCW), passing Grindley Brook Farm on your right. The footpath bends right and passes to the right of a grass hillock. As you round the other side of the hillock, the canal is to your far left. Go over the stile at the bottom of the hill,

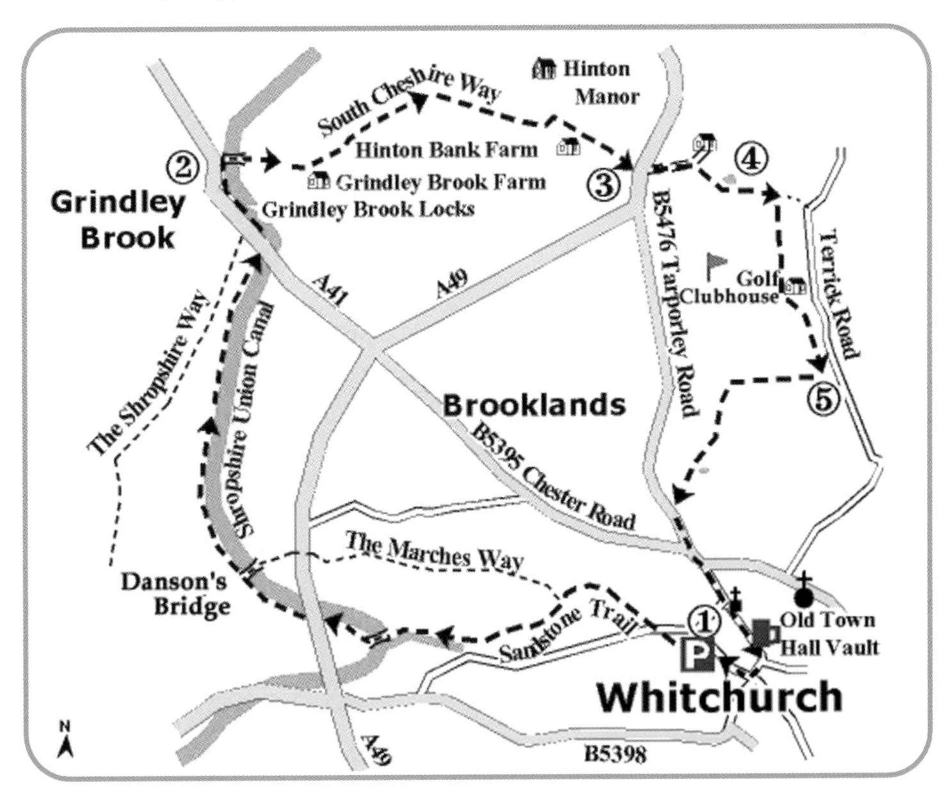

and now head right up a hedged track, still following the waymarkers for the SCW. (The track can be a little muddy after wet weather, but is otherwise good.) After curving left, you will reach a stile on the left, which you go over, aiming for a farm gate set to the left of Hinton Bank Farm. Go through this and follow the driveway down to the B5476 (Tarporley) road.

3 Cross over the road with care, and bear slightly left to meet the tarmac driveway opposite. Just before reaching the trees on the right, turn right over a pair of stiles to arrive on the course of the Hill Valley Golf Club. Head left up the bank, keeping off the course fairway, and walk up the course footpath until you reach a pool, where you are likely to see ducks, moorhens and coots at play.

4 At the pool, bear right, away from the course footpath, and walk on by the side of a small stream, crossing over the golf course but taking great care not to interfere with play. After walking in this easterly direction for about 350 yards, pass to the left of the garden to a house to reach a lane, where you will see a waymarker on the fingerpost outside the club grounds. Go into the grounds, and now bear left onto a course footpath, walking in a southerly direction. Walk to the right of the clubhouse, which you will soon reach, and continue southwards along the pathway, past a waymarker post.

5 As you approach some houses, bear right and continue along the pathway. In about 250 yards, bear left by a teeing-off area. Go over a stile that is set back in the hedge, and head down the left-hand side

Grindley Brook lock

of pastureland, going over the next three fields. Soon after, go over a stile and through a hand-gate by a large pond area. Continue, now walking along the right edge of the field, until you reach the B5476 (Tarporley) road on the edge of Whitchurch. Head left down the road to a traffic island. Go ahead, along the road bearing left onto the London road. Continue into Bargates to reach the church at the top of the High Street. Continue down the High Street, and you will find the Old Town Hall Vault in St Mary's Street just behind the town hall. When you near the bottom of the High Street, turn right up Pepper Street; as you reach the top of the street, you will find the car park on the left.

Place of Interest

Whitchurch Heritage Centre, 12 St Mary's Street, houses various exhibitions (some interactive) relating to the town and its history. The centre also incorporates Whitchurch Craft Centre, where various craftsmen can be seen at work. Telephone: 01948 665432.

Date walk completed:

....

Wenlock Edge 11 Walk

The George and Dragon

The countryside around Much Wenlock is a delightful area to walk in. Starting in this attractive town – with a stroll through its charming streets and a chance to enjoy the pleasing mix of architecture, ranging from medieval to Georgian and Victorian – the journey takes you on through beautiful countryside, with an exhilarating climb up Wenlock Edge, before returning to the town. On the return, you pass the spectacular 12th and 13th-century ruins – including the remains of the church and claustral buildings – of Wenlock Priory, which belongs to the Cluniac order.

The **George and Dragon** dates back to 1700. It has a reputation among locals and visitors alike for excellent food and beer. Jacket potatoes, rarebits, ploughman's and tasty sandwiches and baguettes are on offer, together with main dishes such as sirloin steak, and home-baked ham. Ask about the fascinating ghost story of the large black dog that is said to guard the precious beer in the lower cellar.

Opening times *are from 12 noon to 3 pm and from 6 pm to 11 pm, Monday to Thursday. On Friday and at weekends it is open all day from 12 noon to 11 pm (10.30 pm on Sunday). Food is served from 12 noon to 2 pm and from 6 pm to 9 pm.*

Telephone: *01952 727312.*

Distance: *3½ miles*

OS Explorers 217 and 241
GR 623998

An easy walk in gentle countryside

Starting point: The car park at the back of the George and Dragon in High Street.

How to get there: Much Wenlock is on the A5223, 10 miles south of Telford.

The Walk

1 From the car park, go along the covered footpath of George Shut into High Street, where you will arrive almost opposite the Corn Exchange. Turn left, and stroll along the historic street, passing Raynald's Mansion (17th-century) and the Talbot Inn (14th-century). Continue past Back Lane and Ashfield Hall; then, just past King Street, is Squatters' Cottage, a 17th-century dwelling with a wonderful chimney stack. Continue past the road junction with the B4378 (Bridgnorth) road and into Victoria Road. In a short distance, bear left into Stretton Road, and then turn right up Blakeway Hollow (behind the Horse and Jockey pub). In about 200 yards, go over a stile on the right and walk on the clearly defined footpath over pastureland, gently climbing to a hand gate. Continue to the right of the field hedge, passing by a farm barn before going through a gate, and then crossing a field and a farm track to another hand gate. Soon you will be entering the woodland of Blakeway Hollow.

2 After a few yards, turn right (do not go ahead on the track) onto a path that soon meets a main track in the woods. Turn right along this track to reach the A458 road at the top of Harley Bank.

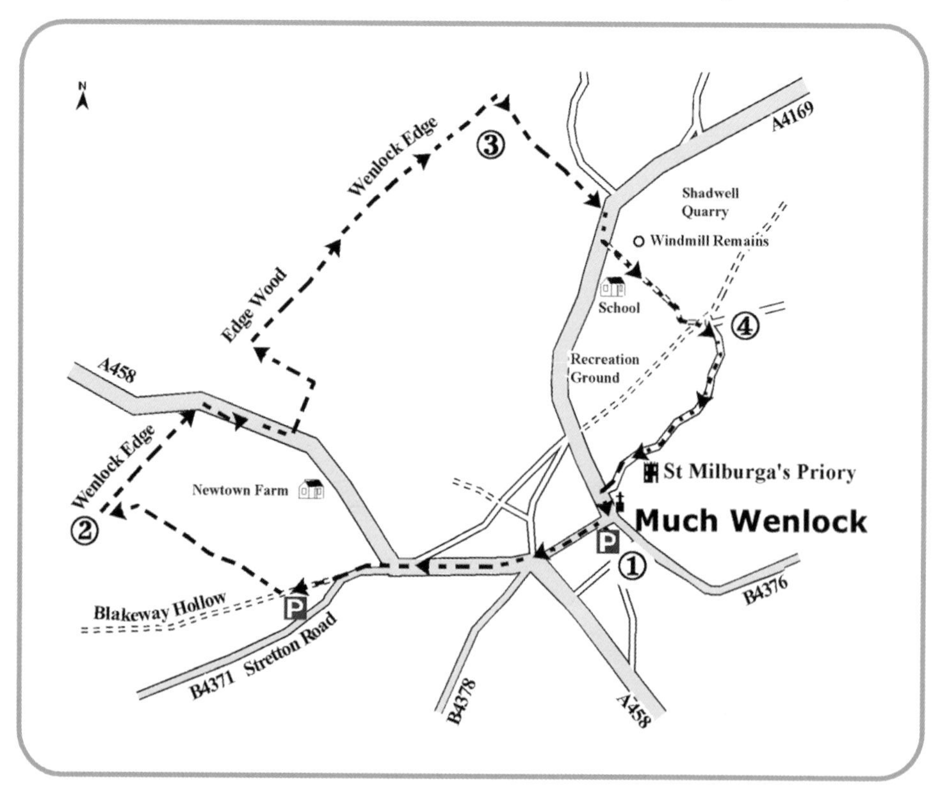

The half-timbered Guildhall and Holy Trinity church

Turn right and walk along the side of the road for about 200 yards; then cross the road with care and go left up a farm track into woodland. When you reach the end of the wood, turn left and climb the footpath along the edge of cultivated fields up to Edge Wood. Now turn right and walk along Wenlock Edge for three quarters of a mile. You will be walking along a clear footpath set to the right of the trees, with a pleasant valley view to the right. As you cross the next six or so fields you will be sheltered by trees on your left. Where the path bends right, enter the trees. (Ahead you will see the huge cooling towers of the power station by the river Severn at Ironbridge Gorge.)

3 Go over the stile at the end of the wood and turn right, walking on the footpath to the left of the field hedge down to the A4169. Turn right and walk along the footway for about 100 yards; then cross the road with care and go through the hand gate opposite. Climb the path up to the ruins of an old windmill, and enjoy the view over the valley to Ash Coppice. From the other side of the windmill, follow the path downhill and through a farm gate, after which it bends left onto a dismantled railway line. Cross the former line (now a local walkway) and climb the steps opposite onto a quiet narrow lane.

4 Go right and follow this lane into Much Wenlock, enjoying the pleasant rural scene with parkland to your right. Soon you will pass (or stop to visit) Wenlock Priory on your left. Continue up the lane, past Priory Hall (built by public subscription as a national school in 1848), and up to Bull Ring, where for hundreds of years bull-baiting took place. (Note the Savings Bank door and the old police station.) Turn left into Wilmore Street and go past Holy Trinity church, pausing to look at the superb half-timbered, 16th-century guildhall. (The information centre is sited in the Wenlock Museum building, the former market hall of 1878, opposite the guildhall.) Turn right into High Street, and then go left through the archway by the George and Dragon to return to the car park.

Place of Interest

Wenlock Priory (English Heritage) has holy wells, shuts, cobbles, whipping posts, stocks and all sorts of Olympic artefacts on this site of St Milburga's abbey, which was founded around AD 680. Telephone: 01952 727466. www.english-heritage.org.uk

Date walk completed:

....

Walk 12 Little Wenlock

The Huntsman

A walk up onto the Wrekin is a special treat indeed. The distinctive 407m hill is a landmark wherever you are in Shropshire and in some places beyond. During my childhood, my parents regularly used the expression *all round the Wrekin*, meaning 'going the long way' or 'not explaining something clearly and directly', and the visit to the impressive hill brought back memories for me. The Wrekin was once the hillfort headquarters of the Celtic Cornovii tribe from the Bronze Age until the 1st century AD. It became part of a royal forest during Saxon and Norman times. The Normans tried to rename the hill Mount Gilbert (after a local hermit), but the local people persisted in calling it the Wrekin and so the name remains today.

Distance: *7 miles*

OS Explorer 242
GR 647070

A hill walk: in parts gently undulating but with a fairly steep ascent and descent of the Wrekin

Starting point: The car park at the Huntsman in Little Wenlock.

How to get there: Little Wenlock is 5½ miles south-west of Telford. Leave Telford on the B5223, and, in about 4 miles, turn right onto local roads, following the signs to Little Wenlock. You will find the Huntsman in the village, on Wellington Road.

The **Huntsman** in Little Wenlock is an unpretentious inn that offers good food in the bar or in the well-presented restaurant area, where you can enjoy large plates of reasonably priced offerings, from snacks to fillet steak Diane. Children and dogs (under control) are welcome. There is a large car park with the village play area nearby.

Opening times *are from 12 noon to 11 pm every day. Food is available at any time during this period, except on Monday, when it is not provided at lunchtime.*

Telephone: *01952 505820.*

The Walk

1 Leave the inn car park and head right, up the road towards the Wrekin. In about half a mile, (just before a right bend in the road), look out for a stile on the bank to the left. Pass the stile onto the footpath strolling through a delightful copse of deciduous trees to reach a farm track. Go right, over a stile, and walk on a footpath set to the right of the trees or hedge, climbing gently towards the hill. Go over over another stile to enter the trees below the Wrekin hill.

2 Turn left and follow the wide track inside the woodland edge. After nearly three quarters of a mile of easy walking, with deciduous trees to the left and with conifers on the bank to your right, you will enter more woodland, with a conifer plantation to the left. Soon the main track arcs left towards a gate, and here you bear right.

3 In a further quarter of a mile, bear right up a permissive path into the woodland on the bank (you are likely to enjoy a bluebell bonanza in spring). The track (a fire break) bends left, and then, where the tracks cross, you turn right. The way arcs gently right, soon to arrive at a

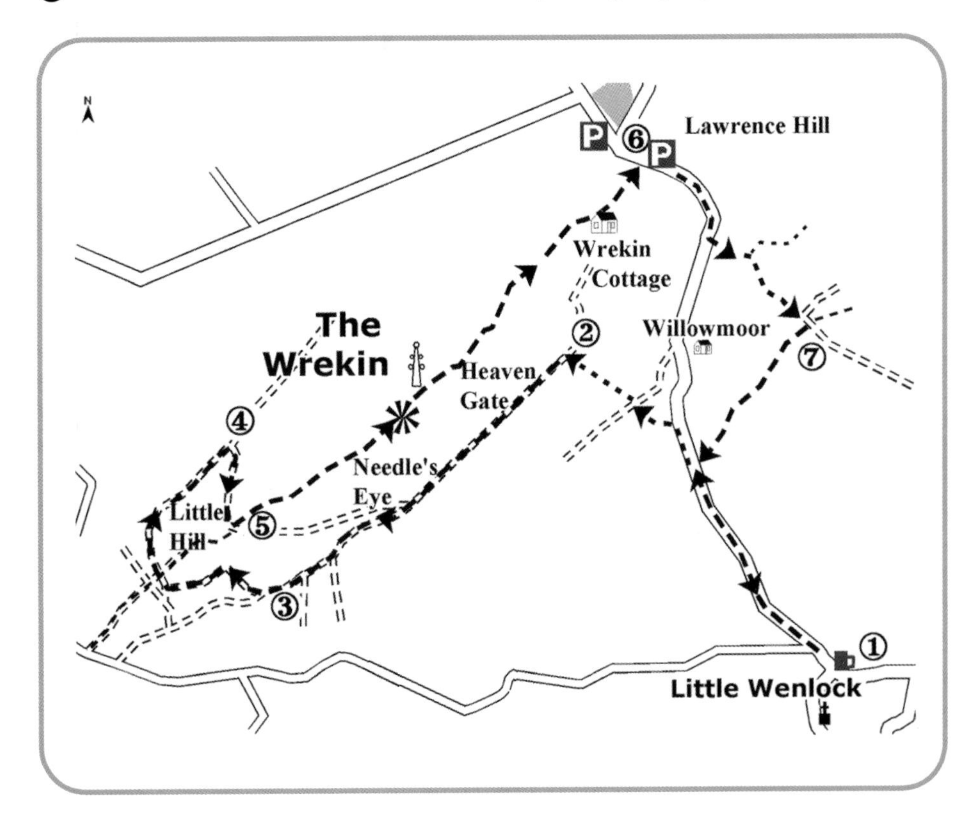

T-junction with a main track. Turn right and keep to the main track for the next 550 yards.

4 Just after ascending into the trees turn right and go up another permissive path that leads to more open ground. (There is a good view to the right over a new plantation of conifers.) Keep to this main track, which curls left around the side of The Wrekin, until you reach a junction.

5 Turn left, and now begin a steep ascent towards the summit of The Wrekin. After about 600 yards, you will arrive by the Needle's Eye and can pause to regain your breath and enjoy a superb view embracing the power station near Ironbridge, and Wenlock Edge. Resume the climb up the hill until you reach the trig point at 407m, where there are further impressive views to be experienced. Continue along the well-used track over the top of the hill. You will pass a communication tower and go between the large boulders of Heaven Gate, where the view to the north is quite outstanding. Now you begin to descend, at first along a good track. (In the autumn the tree colours are superb.) Then, walking down a steep pathway through trees, pass to the left of Wrekin Cottage. After about a quarter of a mile of steep descent, you will meet a main track coming in from the right. Turn left onto it, and soon you will arrive at the main car park.

6 Go onto the road and turn right to pass another car park, set in an old quarry to the left. Continue up the quiet road for the next 600 yards. Where the road bends right, turn left on the corner to climb a wide tarmac track; in about 500 yards you will reach a junction of tracks.

Heaven Gate

7 Turn right onto a good farm track, and then, in 25 yards, turn right again into the trees. The clear footpath soon emerges along the right-hand edge of the trees, where you can enjoy fleeting glimpses of The Wrekin to your right. Leave the trees, maintaining your line over a couple of fields and stiles until you reach the road. Here turn left and retrace your steps to the Huntsman, where well earned refreshments await.

Place of Interest

Ironbridge, 5½ miles to the south-east, boasts a wonderful bridge over the river Severn and is famous as the birthplace of the Industrial Revolution. Telephone: 01952 432166.

Date walk completed:

....

Cleehill

The Kremlin

Titterstone Clee Hill, at 533m, the highest summit in Shropshire and one of its famous landmarks, is explored on this exceptionally fine hill walk. The area has been extensively mined, and there are quarries still to be seen.

Distance: *8 miles*

OS Explorer 203
GR 595756

A hill walk on generally good footpaths and tracks, but some boggy areas in wet weather

Starting point: The car park at The Kremlin, Cleehill

How to get there: Cleehill is on the A4117 road, about 6½ miles east of Ludlow.

The **Kremlin**, earlier called the Craven Arms, was renamed the Kremlin about 18 years ago at the time when the radio station on Titterstone Clee Hill ceased to monitor information emanating from Moscow. Today, a warm welcome and superb home cooked food awaits you. The large steaks and traditional Sunday roast are particularly popular. There can be few greater pleasures in life than to sup a pint with an appetizing meal while admiring the fine view from the pub veranda.

Opening times *are from 11.30 am to 11 pm. Food is available between 12 noon and 2 pm (except on Tuesdays).*

Telephone: *01584 890950.*

The Walk

1 From the car park, follow the tarmac track at the back of the inn and walk along the footpath to the right of the communication tower. Once over the wall by the buildings, go left over a stile, and then head left (west), crossing a couple of farm fields and going over another stile. (There is an outstanding view ahead of you.) At the next stile, continue ahead; go through a wall gap and then turn left to go down the hill on a footpath that emerges onto the driveway by Prospect Cottage. Turn right and go down to the former railway; then head right along the track, passing by a former loading area, to arrive by houses. Remain on the dismantled railway track and bend left to come to a country road. Turn right and walk up the road for about 15 yards; then turn left and continue down the dismantled line/driveway.

2 After about 250 yards, turn right and go over a stile into pastureland, joining the Shropshire Way. Head for a farm gate in the far left-hand corner. Then continue along a well-walked footpath to another farm gate. Here, the path goes right, up the side of the field edge, for about 150 yards, and then veers sharp left to reach a stile below Nine Springs Farm. Go over this and the footbridge over a stream, and continue along a fern-lined grass footpath. Cross over the tarmac driveway and continue along the grass footpath up to a raised stretch of land called the Titterstone Incline. Go up this lovely grass track and turn right. Walk to the car park on Titterstone Clee Hill.

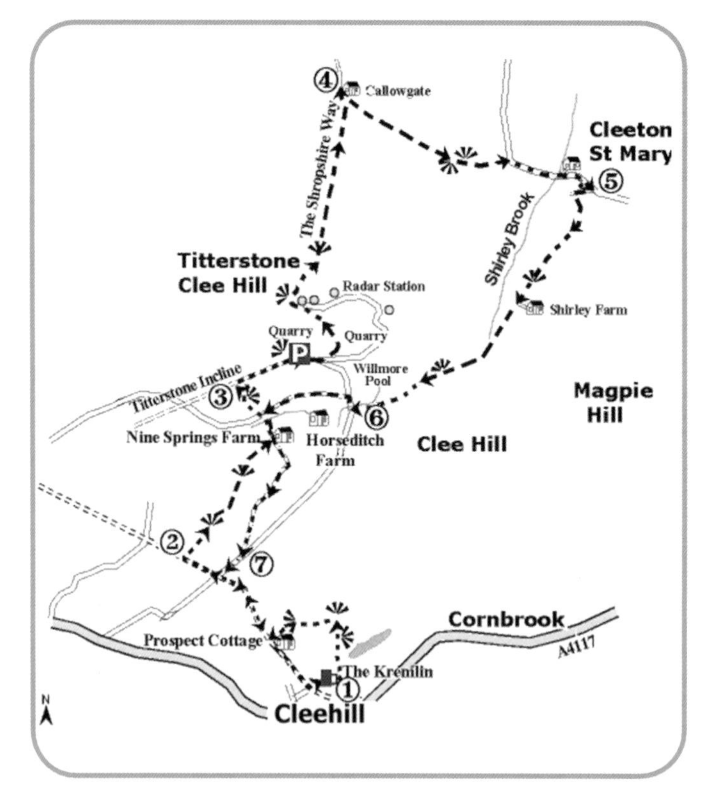

3 Turn right through the gates (closed to vehicles) into the radar station complex. Go left immediately inside the gates and climb up the Shropshire Way. Bear left at the first quarry and ascend to the very top of the hill, passing close to a couple of radar dishes (the impressive white domes are to the right), to reach the trig point. The path loops right around the top of the hill, and then, when nearly level with the large white communication dome, it bends left, descending in a generally northerly direction towards Brown Clee Hill (540m). Soon you will reach a gate by Callowgate farmhouse.

Nine Springs Farm below Titterstone Clee Hill

4 Do not go through the gate but go sharp right to leave the Shropshire Way and walk south-eastwards by the Callowgate fence. Although lacking waymarkers, a footpath exists to the right of a farm fence. In about three quarters of a mile, the footpath curves left to a lane by a cattle grid. Go right along the lane, crossing the bridge over Shirley Brook before coming into Cleeton St Mary.

5 Just past St Mary's church, bear right and walk by the metal fence to the churchyard. When you reach the church gate, go left (just after the last house in the village) and climb up the hill opposite, keeping to the right of the hedge (Titterstone Clee Hill is to your right). Walk on this path for the next 1¼ miles (Magpie Hill will be to your left). Follow the path as it bends right and descends to a quiet road by a small bridge.

6 Go right along the road for about 100 yards, then turn left. Go down a tarmac track past Horseditch Farm, and continue to the footbridge on the left that you crossed on the outward journey. Follow the Shropshire Way waymarkers, but this time go through the gateway by Nine Springs Farm and go along the farm drive (a public footpath). After going through a farm gate, the drive bends sharp right. After almost half a mile of lovely walking you arrive at a road.

7 Turn right and go down the road to reach houses. Turn left by Hedgehog Cottage and retrace your steps past the former loading area of the dismantled railway. Continue along the track, passing Prospect Cottage, to arrive in the village of Cleehill. When opposite a dead end road (on the right), turn left up a track and follow it as it bends generally right, to arrive, through a farm gate, back in the car park of the Kremlin.

Place of Interest

Ludlow, 6 miles to the east, is an architectural gem, with a superb castle and many medieval and Georgian buildings. Visit www.thisisludlow.co.uk for more details.

Date walk completed:

....

Walk 14 Eardington, near Bridgnorth

The Halfway House Inn

Setting out from Eardington, the walk goes across typical Shropshire countryside before passing the waterwheel at Daniel's Mill (the largest working waterwheel powering a cornmill in England) on the way to the banks of the river Severn, where a delightful stroll awaits. The route then crosses the Severn Valley railway line before ascending gently up through Eardington. There is an opportunity to visit and explore the beautiful town of Bridgnorth, with its many half-timbered buildings, market, shops and inns. Sitting high on a sandstone cliff, the town is divided in two: a high town and low town, while in the valley below the Severn river winds its way through the countryside. There are caves, a castle, and a cliff railway, and, from the high town, spectacular views of the valley and low town.

Distance: *4½ miles*

OS Explorer 218
GR 708908

An easy walk with some undulations

Starting point: The car park at the Halfway House Inn, but please seek permission from the landlord.

How to get there: Take the B4363 from Bridgnorth. The Halfway House Inn is on the right, in about 1½ miles.

The **Halfway House Inn,** a 16th-century coaching inn, was originally called the Red Lion. It owes its present name to Queen Victoria. In 1823 she was travelling between Pitchford Hall, near Shrewsbury and Great Witley Court, Worcestershire and stopped here to change horses. When she asked where she was, she was told she was 'halfway there', and thereafter the pub became known as the Halfway House.

Opening times *are Monday to Friday 8 am to 11 pm (Monday 9 am); Saturday 8 am to 12 midnight and Sunday 9 am to 6 pm. Food is served from 12 noon to 2 pm every day (until 3 pm Sunday) and from 6 pm to 9 pm.*

Telephone: *01746 768063.*

The Walk

❶ From the car park, turn right and go along Cleobury Road to a road junction. Turn right and go up a quiet lane for about 200 yards. Just after passing a white cottage, turn left and go over a stile, following the waymarker direction to a second stile into trees and past Potseething spring. Continue across two more fields, and then go over a further stile onto a track in the village of Oldbury. In about 100 yards, just past a cottage, turn right and follow a hedged footpath, crossing another track to continue along a further narrow hedged footpath set to the right of a cottage. A stile takes you into pastureland, which you cross to another stile. Go over this and turn left along a driveway. Pass through the farm-style gate, and then turn right to continue on a final hedged footpath. A stile leads into open land; here follow the clear footpath down to a stile by the hedge in the far corner.

Go into the trees and cross two footbridges over the stream to reach a wider stretch of water. Bear right and walk on the grass footpath to the right of the main pool. Go beneath Daniel Bridge, which carries the Severn Valley railway. (You may be lucky enough to see a steam

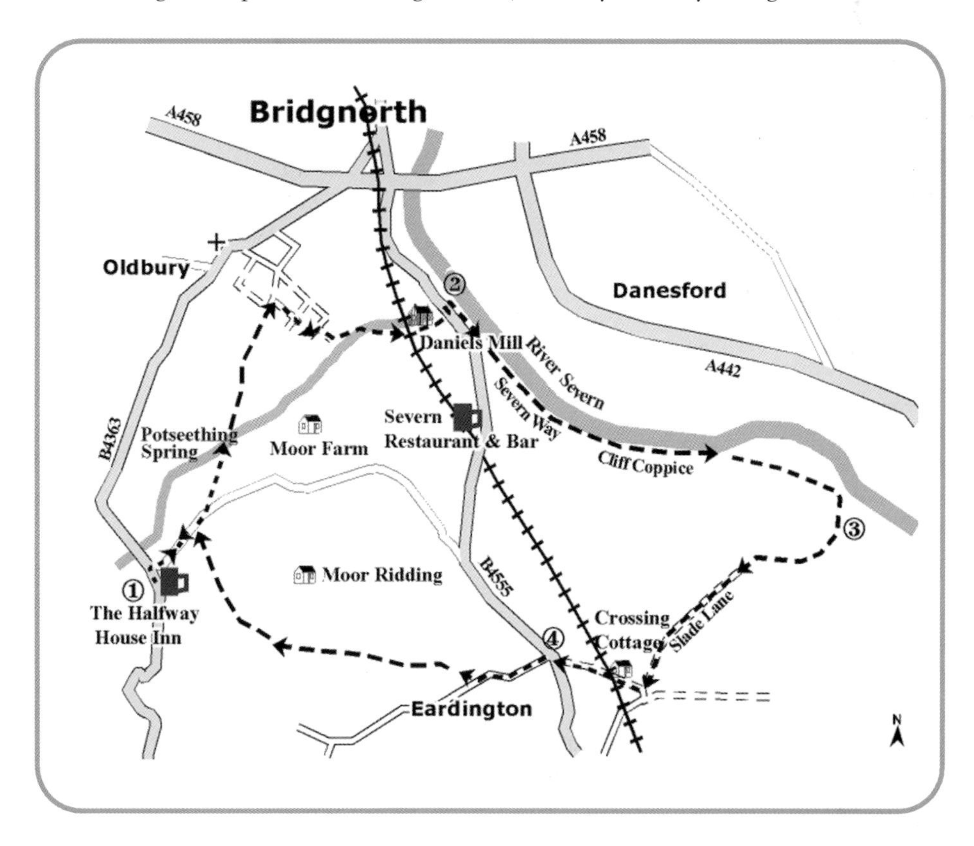

train cross over the bridge.) The route goes to the right of Daniel's Mill and down its main driveway to reach the B4555. Here, go left for about 25 yards, and then turn right through a gap in the fence to walk down to the banks of the river Severn and the Severn Way footpath.

2 Turn right and walk on the Severn Way for almost a mile. This will take you along the banks of the mighty river and below Cliff Coppice. As you leave the trees over a stile, bear right, and continue walking to the left of a bank of trees and then a wire fence. The path bends right, and ahead you will see sewage works.

3 At the field corner, go right over a stile and walk up the clear footpath (farm track) that climbs and arcs gently right between hills and to the left of a clump of trees. Follow the track as it curves left; soon you will be walking on a good farm track called Slade Lane. After 600 yards, you will reach some deciduous trees; turn right here and follow the grass track set to the right of the trees. Soon you will arrive at the railway line by Crossing Cottage. Cross the line and walk up the track opposite to reach the B4555 in Eardington.

Daniel's Mill

4 Turn right, and then left up the road opposite. About 125 yards after passing a lovely old school building with a bell tower, turn right over a stile and walk in a north-westerly direction on the clear pathway across the large field. Maintain your direction over several fields and stiles, following the waymarker direction. Soon you will arrive on the road near to the white cottage you passed at the start of the walk. Turn left and retrace your steps to the Halfway House Inn.

Date walk completed:

....

Places of Interest

The Severn Valley Railway travels between Bridgnorth and Kidderminster. Telephone: 01299 403816.

Daniel's Mill in Eardington has a huge waterwheel powering a working cornmill. Telephone: 01746 762753.

Dudmaston Hall (National Trust) is a superb late 17th-century country mansion with an art collection and lakeside gardens. Telephone: 01746 780866.

Cheswardine

The Wharf Tavern

Starting from Cheswardine, this attractive walk takes you down to the Shropshire Union canal and then along country lanes and footpaths into open countryside, passing through a couple of 'drumbles' (copses) before returning to the village along a good track. Cheswardine stands on a small hill, with the church of St Swithun sitting proudly at its top. The Shropshire Union canal passes to the west of the village; in the neighbouring parish, it enters Woodseaves cutting, which is over a mile in length and 90 feet deep, a mini man-made canyon carved through the countryside.

Distance: *4 miles*

OS Explorer 243
GR 719297

An easy walk

Starting point: The main road in Cheswardine. Please park with consideration.

How to get there: Cheswardine is situated 5 miles south-east of Market Drayton, on the border with Staffordshire.

Situated beside the canal, at bridge 55, the **Wharf Tavern** offers moorings and attractive canal-side gardens. Few things can be pleasanter than sitting in the Wharf Tavern gardens for Sunday lunch, enjoying one of the reasonably priced roasts (cooked to perfection) and watching the canal world go by. The grill room offers steaks, with a good selection of alternatives on the menu, and bar meals and sandwiches can be enjoyed in the pleasant lounge. Well-behaved children are welcome. There is a large car park.

Opening times *are from 12 noon to 3 pm and from 6.30 pm to 11 pm. Food is served between 12 noon and 2 pm and from 6.30 pm to 9 pm.*

Telephone: *01680 661226.*

The Walk

❶ From the main street in Cheswardine, turn down Symond's Way (passing the interesting awards given to the village in the large village competition); at the end, turn left into Copelea, and, just after number 34, go right down a fenced path to reach open land at the back of the bungalows. Turn right and go along the path at the back of the houses; cross a stile onto Haywood Lane. Turn left and walk along this quiet lane for about 300 yards; then turn left, going over another stile and across pastureland, walking to the left of the hedge. After going over several stiles, you will arrive in a plantation of young trees. You need to aim southwards, but you may find it easier to go left and walk along the grass area, circling to the left of the plantation. Soon you will reach a hedge opening; you will see a canal bridge through the trees, and should aim for this. Go over the bridge, and drop down to the right to reach the towpath of the Shropshire Union canal.

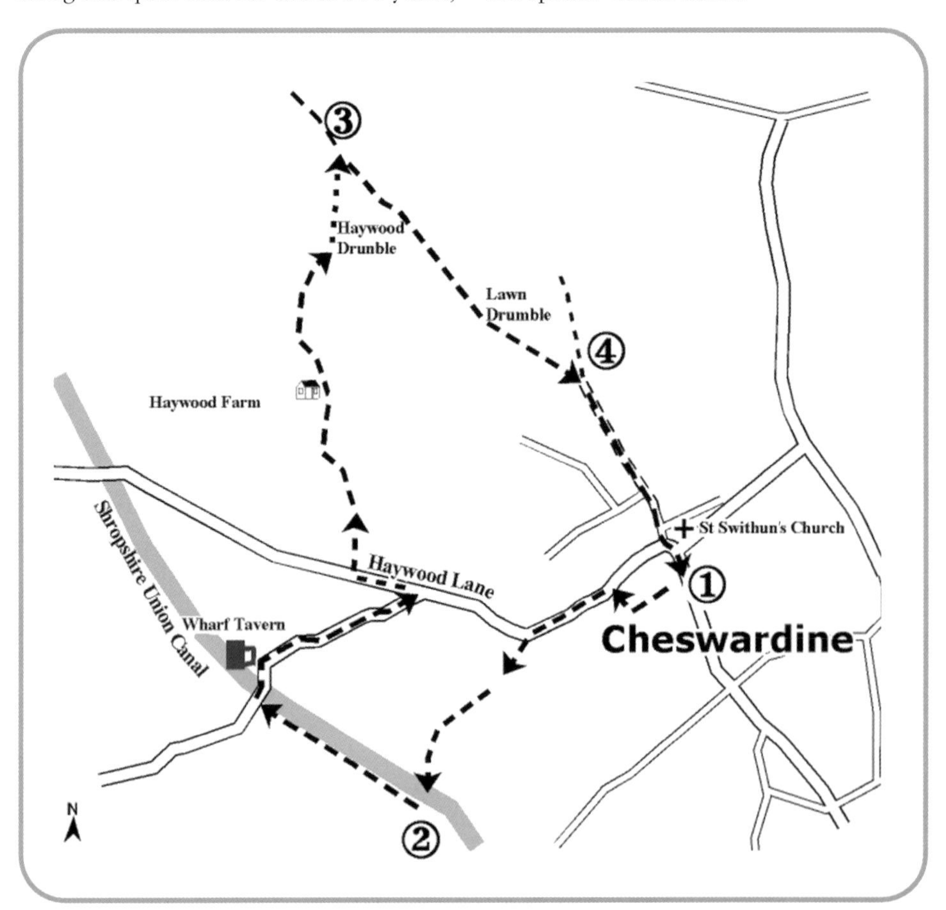

2 Go left along the towpath. In about 400 yards you will reach Goldstone canal bridge. Go up to the road; cross over the bridge, passing the Wharf Tavern Inn; and continue up the lane until you reach the road junction with Haywood Lane. Turn left, and walk along the grass verge for 250 yards. Now turn right through a farm gate and cross a cultivated field towards woodland. At the far side of the field, a stile will lead you around the top of the woodland. At its end, bear left, and walk to the right of the field hedge for the next 100 yards until you reach an oak tree. Cross the cultivated field, aiming for a stile set to the right of the brick part of the Haywood farm complex. Over the stile, pass between the farm buildings onto a grass track, which you follow for about 200 yards. Then, just past some trees, bear right, and go across another cultivated field, aiming for a stile on the edge of Haywood Drumble. Go through the trees and over the stile at the far end. Walk on the clear footpath to the far left-hand corner of the next field. (You will see the building of Cheswardine Park Farm over the hedge ahead.)

Taking a rest at Cheswardine

3 At the field corner, turn sharp right and walk on the footpath, to the right of the field hedge. A stile leads into the woodland of Haywood Drumble, and, after negotiating a footpath through the trees, you will emerge in another cultivated field. Continue along the footpath set to the left of the hedge until you arrive by the trees of Lawn Drumble. At the woodland, turn left for about 10 yards; then turn right and enter the trees. Walk through the attractive woodland on the clear footpath that seems to run almost parallel with the right edge of the trees. A stile will take you into another large cultivated field, which you cross on the clear footpath to a group of trees.

4 Turn right onto a hedged track beside the trees and walk to its end. (You can enter the woodland, if you prefer, and stroll along the clear, well-used footpath inside, which runs almost parallel with the track.) Soon you will pass between several large stones and arrive near St Swithun's church in Cheswardine.

Place of Interest
Hodnet Hall, just over 7½ miles to the west, has been the home of the Heber-Percy family for several centuries. It has superb gardens to visit. Telephone: 01630 685786.

Date walk completed:

....

Walk 16 Norbury

The Junction Inn

The figure-of-eight route of this easy walk through attractive Staffordshire countryside takes you along part of the Shropshire Union canal, and you have the opportunity to see the unique telegraph pole bridge – it is the sole survivor of the many telegraph lines which once existed on the banks of canals throughout the country.

Distance: *7 miles*

OS Explorer 243
GR 793228

An easy walk along good footpaths and the towpath of the Shropshire Union canal

Starting point: The car park of the Junction Inn at Norbury.

How to get there: Norbury is 6½ miles south-west of Eccleshall. Take the A519 towards Newport. In 6 miles, turn left onto local roads to arrive in Norbury.

The **Junction Inn** is a favourite with canal users and walkers alike. What a pleasure it is to sit at one of the benches at the canalside, watching the world of narrow-boats arriving for lunch. You will receive a warm welcome and traditional home-made food from bar snacks through to grills. Large portions of steak pie are the favourite of many, and there is a Sunday carvery.

Opening times *are all day throughout the year. Food is available every day between 1 pm and 6 pm.*

Telephone: *01785 284288.*

The Walk

1 From the inn car park, head left up the road. At the T-junction, turn right and walk along the pavement through the village of Norbury. In about 650 yards, turn right up a quiet road past the village hall to arrive, in 250 yards, at the A519. Cross over the road with care, and continue up the road opposite, towards Loynton. After about 450 yards of easy walking, the road descends to a junction by the Millennium Boulder Trail sign.

2 Here, turn right and walk along the good grass track. After curving left, the track arcs gently right, towards the trees near Rue Hill, which you enter to arrive at Double Culvert Bridge (no. 40).

3 Cross the bridge over the canal and continue through the copse on the far bank, leaving through a hand gate. Then walk on the path going north-east over several fields, passing to the left of buildings and then to the right of a sycamore tree. After following this field path for about half a mile, you reach a car repair area. Bear left through it, and then walk to the left of a field hedge, going generally north-west. In about 325 yards, go over a stile onto a lane, and turn left along the lane, passing Hollow Farm. At the first bend in the road, bear left through a gate and cross a stile into pastureland, walking on the clear waymarked path. Keep to the left of the hedge; then go through a hedge gap and over a couple of stiles to reach Grub Street. Turn right to arrive in the peaceful village of High Offley, which is overlooked by the 700-year-old church imperiously set on a hilltop. At the road junction, bear left through the village, and, in about 250 yards, go left

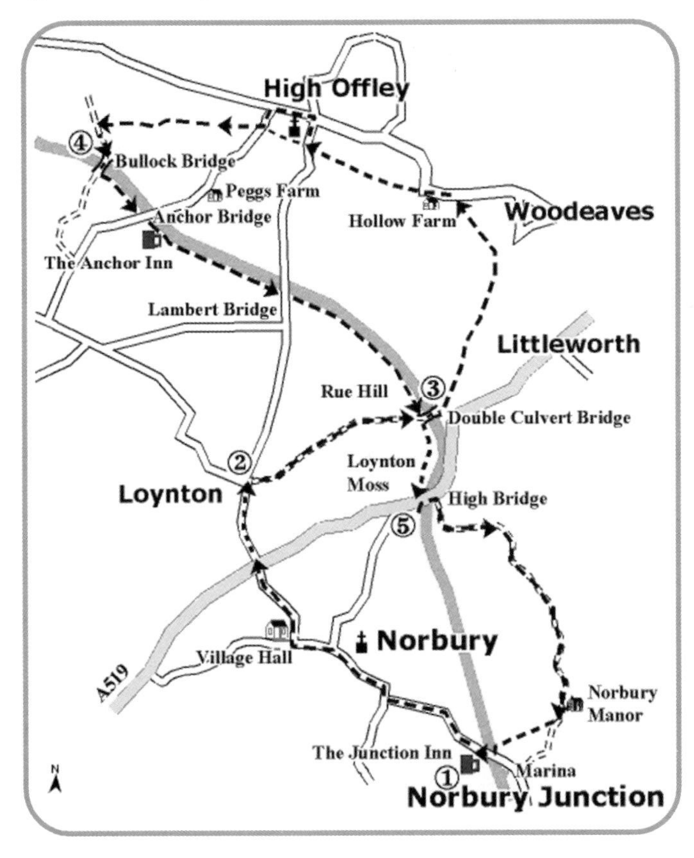

down Pegg Lane. In just over 100 yards, turn right over a stile, keeping to the left of the field hedge. Go through the corner gate; then cross over a footbridge before walking across a further field to reach its hedge. Now turn left again, and, in 150 yards, go right onto a wide track that leads to Bullock Bridge and the Shropshire Union canal.

On the route near Norbury Manor

❹ Cross the bridge and go down to the canal towpath; then walk along the towpath, going south-east. Pass beneath Anchor Bridge (no. 42), and continue past the Anchor Inn and under Lambert Bridge. Leave the canal towpath at Double Culvert Bridge. Then go onto a woodland footpath into Loynton Moss.

The area, now a reserve, was formed in the Ice Age about 10,000 years ago. It is mentioned in the Domesday Book. In the pleasant woodland, you should look out for common and greater reed mace and lesser celandine. You may also spot a sedge warbler or a speckled wood butterfly.

Walk on the clear path through the trees above the Shropshire Union canal. Eventually, you will descend to the A519. (Cross the road, and go down the towpath opposite to get a good view of High Bridge, no. 39, the famous telegraph bridge.)

❺ Walk back to the road and turn right over the canal bridge. Turn right and walk along the bridleway set to the left of trees. The track heads in an easterly direction at first, and then bends right, going generally south-east, to continue to the right of woodland. At the corner of the wood, turn right and follow a track towards Norbury Manor. You will pass to the left of a small moat and then by the large manor house. About 50 yards beyond the house, turn right and walk the clear footpath across a large cultivated field to arrive on the Norbury Junction canal bridge. Climb the steps onto the canal bridge; from here you can enjoy a fine view of the marina and the Junction Inn.

Place of Interest

Eccleshall, 6½ miles to the north-east, has 57 listed or historical buildings, and there is a fascinating town trail to follow. Leaflets are available from the town's library in the High Street. Telephone: 01785 851024; www.eccleshallguide.com.

Date walk completed:

....

Kinver 17 Walk

The Vine

A scenic circuit follows the towpath of the Staffordshire and Worcestershire canal between Kinver and Stewponey locks. It then passes through a pretty bluebell wood by the side of the meandering river Stour. There are pleasant views to enjoy on the walk, which ends with a stroll along Kinver's fascinating High Street. Kinver, recorded as Chenevare in the Domesday Book, is renowned as a centre for fine walking. There are a number of buildings of interest to enjoy, some in the High Street dating back to medieval times. The White Hart Hotel and the pharmacy are two of the buildings which helped the village to win an Architectural Heritage Award in 1975. Kinver Grammar School is a 16th-century, half-timbered building, no longer used as a school. St Peter's church on the hill overlooking the village is a special place, with its unique 'stained-glass window' lampshade and its fascinating exhibition detailing the history of Kinver. The park area of Kinver Edge offers some 200 acres of superb scenery.

Distance: *4½ miles*

OS Explorer 219
GR 848835

Easy walking on a canal towpath and good paths

Starting point: The car park at the Vine

How to get there: Kinver is 6 miles south-west of Kingswinford, near to Dudley. Take the A4101 (Summer Hill) out of Kingswinford and, in about a mile, turn left onto the A449. In Stourton, turn right onto the A458, and, in about a mile, turn left into Hyde Lane to arrive in Kinver. Drive down the High Street, and bear left into Mill Lane to find the Vine.

Once you have discovered the **Vine** it will become a favourite, for there can be few nicer ways to enjoy a summer lunchtime or evening than to lounge in its garden, with a drink in hand, watching beautifully decorated barges negotiate the adjacent canal lock. Built in 1771 for the workers on James Brindley's meandering contour canal, the attractive building is adorned with colourful hanging flower baskets in summer. As well as bar snacks, there is an impressive à la carte menu including dishes such as exotic mushroom pancakes with mornay sauce and cheddar glaze, and steak and kidney pie made with Enville ale.

Opening times *are from noon to 11 pm each day. Food is served between noon and 2 pm and from 6.30 pm to 10 pm during the week; at weekends it is available at any time during opening hours.*

Telephone: *01384 877291.*

The Walk

1 From the Vine inn, turn right and cross Kinver Lock Bridge. Go right again, onto the towpath of the Staffordshire and Worcestershire canal, heading past busy Kinver Lock (no. 29) to reach a mooring area of colourful narrowboats. (The river Stour is close on the left, seemingly about to collide with the canal, but then veering away into the countryside.) After about half a mile, you will reach Hyde Lock (no. 30).

Near it, Hyde Mill, built by Richard Foley in 1629, was the first commercially successful iron slitting mill in England. Powered by the river Stour, it was one of a dozen forges and steel mills which blazed and hammered their products in the area during the Industrial Revolution. The mill became derelict in 1912 and no

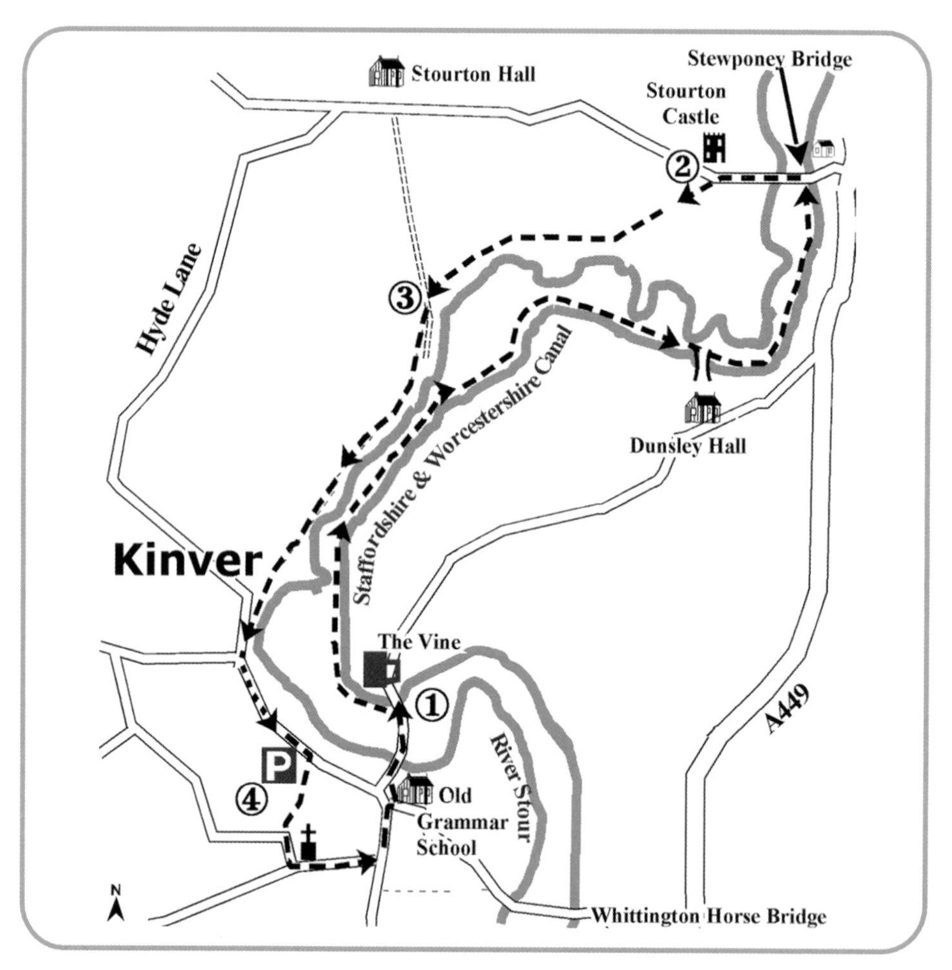

longer exists, although the footings of the mill structures and its boundary walls are still visible.

Soon you will pass through the 25-yard Dunsley Tunnel, where, in 1805, the squire of Dunsley Hall was attacked by a highwayman as he returned from selling cattle at Kidderminster market. He managed to crawl back to Dunsley Hall, where he died. The highwayman was caught at Whittington Inn and was the last man to be publicly hanged and gibbeted at nearby Gibbet Wood.

The towpath again draws very close to the river and then passes beneath Stewponey Bridge to arrive at Stewponey lock (no. 31), where you will find a photo opportunity and a small souvenir shop. Leave the lock area, ascending to the pavement and cross the bridge over the river.

2 Walk beside the road for about 200 yards, and, opposite the castellated gate entrance to Stourton Castle, go left through a kissing gate. Go down the clear path over a cultivated field, pausing to enjoy a good view of the countryside. A stile leads into attractive woodland, and, in spring, you will pass a carpet of bluebells as you walk along the footpath by a wire fence, soon to emerge by Hyde Farm cottages.

3 Bear left along the clear waymarked path, that takes you over pastureland with the Stour close by on your left. (On the approach to Kinver, there is a clear view of St Peter's church on the hill ahead.) Pass between the leisure buildings and the bowling green and miniature railway, and then continue along a tarmac lane to

A lock on the Staffordshire & Worcestershire canal

reach Kinver. Turn left and go along the High Street.

4 Enter the car park at the rear of the post office and climb the steep zigzag footpath to visit St Peter's church. Take time to enjoy the fine view from the churchyard wall, and then leave the churchyard through the main gates into Church Hill. Turn left and go down the hill to Cookley Lane. Here, turn left and descend towards Kinver. In about 100 yards, turn right into Dark Lane to view the magnificent half-timbered medieval grammar school, which functioned as a school for almost 400 years, until 1915. Go down the narrow lane to the left of the old school, passing between natural sandstone walls, to reach Mill Lane; then turn right to cross the river and stroll back to the Vine Inn.

Place of Interest

Himley Hall, seven miles north-west of Kinver, is a great Palladian mansion set in 180 acres of grounds designed by 'Capability' Brown. Telephone: 01902 32665/324093.

Date walk completed:

....

Walk **18** *Hill Top*

The Rose & Crown

An attractive amble around the lovely reservoir of Knypersley Pool is included in this walk, which then passes through tranquil woodland before strolling over heather-covered Marshes Hill Common into Hill Top and Brown Edge. The footpath then descends over pastureland, and you walk beside a feeder canal on the way to Knypersley Mill and back to the car park.

Distance: *4½ miles*

OS Explorer 258
GR 894550

An undulating walk on country park pathways and on good footpaths

Starting point: The Knypersley Pool car park in Greenway Bank Country Park.

How to get there: Hill Top is some 7 miles north of Stoke on Trent. Leave Stoke on the A52. At Baddeley Green, bear right onto the A53/A5009. In a further 1½ miles, turn left onto local roads and follow the signs for Greenway Bank Country Park.

Built in the 1600s, the **Rose & Crown**, is a friendly pub, that has a good selection of food, including a vegetarian choice. There is a specials board, offering scrumptious pies and haddock.

Opening times *are 12 noon to 11 pm daily. Food is available between 12 noon and 8 pm. It is a popular place on Sundays; so booking is advisable.*

Telephone: *01782 503375.*

The Walk

1 From the car park, walk on the wide tarmac pathway along the left margin of the serpentine lake for about 100 yards. Turn right, go down an embankment, and turn right. Continue with the lake to your right. After about 200 yards, the pathway bends right; in a further 200 yards, look out for a stepped path going off to the left. Ascend the steps, passing the Warder's Tower, and continue up the Staffordshire Moorlands Walk footpath heading northwards out of the trees. The footpath continues to the left of hedges and wire fences, passing through a metal hand-gate with a view to your left that includes Mow Top Castle. At the top of the gentle but long ascent, go over the stile onto a farm track. Turn left and walk up the track as far as Knypersley Park farm buildings.

2 Do not go onto the lane, but turn right before the hedge and walk along the footpath through the trees to a stone wall. Just inside the low wall, the footpath descends along the edge of a wood of young oak and sweet beech. After crossing a couple of stiles, arc left along

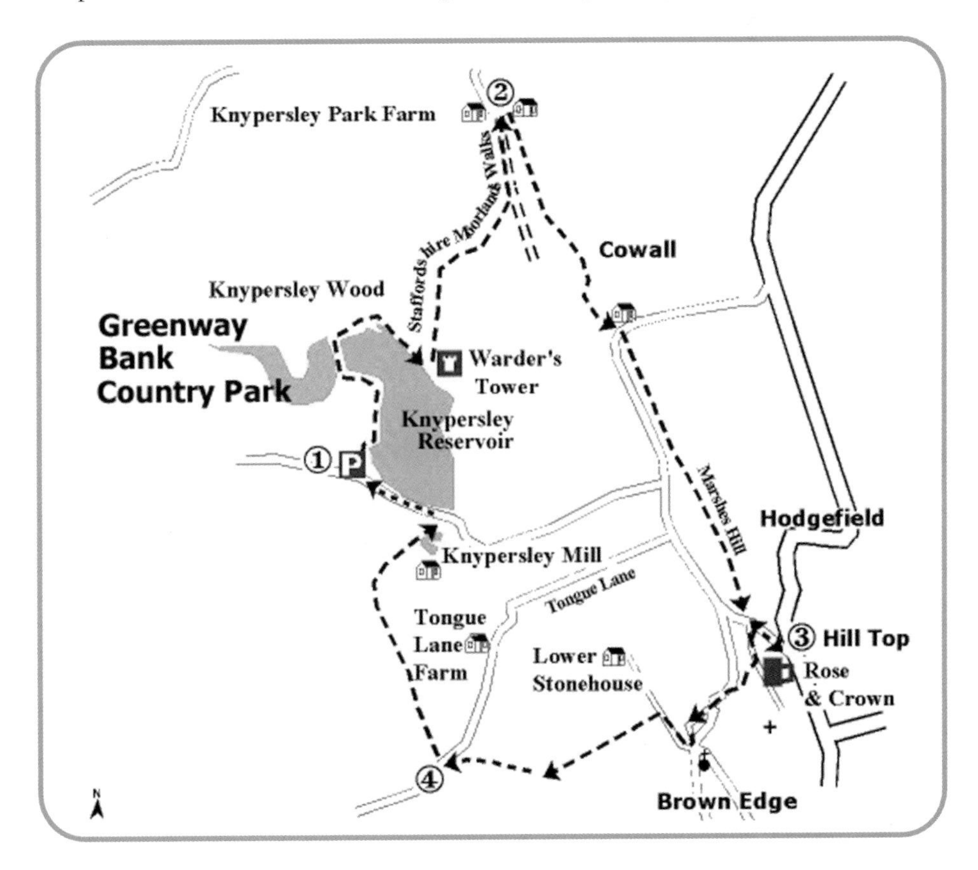

the path and descend by the side of a stream; then climb a bank, passing to the right of a barn and onto a farm driveway. Go over a bridge onto a road. Cross the road, go over the stile opposite, and climb a grass footpath, passing to the left of a cottage to arrive on the edge of Marshes Hill Common. Ignore the footpath to the right, and continue over the common, through banks of heather. (At the top of the hill you can pause by a bench and enjoy the view from near the toposcope. You should easily be able to pick out the Wrekin to the left, and behind you the Roaches are silhouetted on the skyline.) Drop down to a car park area, and then, to reach the Rose and Crown, bear left up the roadway opposite; the pub is on the right, in about 150 yards.

The Warder's Tower

3 To continue, go ahead along Back Lane, situated opposite the car park. In about 100 yards, head right down a waymarked footpath to the right of a communication mast, passing a cottage, to arrive on New Lane. Turn left and stroll down this quiet road. Where it bends left, turn right into Old Lane. This soon bends left and you will arrive back on New Lane, emerging to enjoy a good view of the church of St Anne. Turn right by the telephone box and head down Boardman's Bank. In about 125 yards, turn left at a fingerpost that leads to a house. Walk on the clear farm track set to the right of the house for the next 300 yards, going over the stile at its end. The footpath arcs right and then left, and you should aim for a stile in the bottom corner of the field to reach Tongue Lane.

4 Cross over the lane, and walk on the clear footpath beside a babbling brook (the head of Trent) and a canal feeder. Maintain your direction for the next 750 yards, going over a series of stiles, with the brook and the feeder canal never far away. The footpath curves right, passing near to Knypersley Mill and then goes left. Climb the steep steps to arrive on the road bridge near to Greenway Bank Country Park. Head left along the side of the road to return to the parking area.

Date walk completed:

....

Place of Interest

Biddulph Grange Gardens (National Trust), six miles north of Hill Top, comprise 15 acres of connected 'compartments', designed in the mid-19th century by James Bateman to form one of the most unusual gardens in Britain. Telephone: 01782 517999.

Brewood

The Admiral Rodney

This delightful walk takes you along the Shropshire Union canal into the attractive medieval village Brewood (pronounced *brood*), a tranquil place, mentioned in the Domesday Book, steeped in history, and full of treasures. Situated in Brewood Forest, the village was visited by several early kings for hunting. It has been a centre of Catholicism since the 16th century, and was closely associated with the escape of Charles II after the battle of Worcester in 1651. Much of its Georgian character has been retained, and in 1969 the area was designated an outstanding conservation area. There is much to explore in Brewood and you will find many interesting buildings. The oldest is Old Smithy Cottages (1350), and there are many 18th-century buildings, including St Dominic's School (1798), the former workhouse, and Speedwell Castle (1740), an ornate neo-Gothic house. The old pump and horse trough in the attractive Market Place mark the site of the parish pump, and here there is a signpost revealing Brewood's significant success in Staffordshire's Best Kept Village competition. The church of St Mary and St Chad contains the altar tombs of the Catholic Giffard family of nearby Chillington Hall.

Distance: *5 miles*

OS Explorer 242
GR 883085

An easy walk along well-marked footpaths and the towpath of the Shropshire Union canal

Starting point: The Admiral Rodney in Dean Street.

How to get there: Brewood is situated about 8 miles north-west of Wolverhampton, just west of Coven, off the A449 (Wolverhampton to Stafford) road.

The **Admiral Rodney** is a well-appointed Victorian pub that extends a warm welcome to walkers in the comfortable lounge bar, where an extensive menu of very good food ranging from snacks to à la carte is available. The many home-cooked specials include toasted baguettes that are a treat for the walker in a hurry. There is a private garden for afternoon teas, which is available for group bookings.

Opening times *are from 11 am to 11 pm, Monday to Saturday, and noon to 10.30 pm on Sunday. Food is served every lunchtime and evening.*

Telephone: *01902 850583.*

The Walk

1 Leave the car park at the Admiral Rodney, turn right, and go up Dean Street. In about 100 yards, by the churchyard of St Mary and St Chad, cross the road and enter a signed footpath between buildings to join the Staffordshire Way. This pleasant path passes between buildings and then bends left, continuing across a couple of fields up to a stile by the side of Dean's Hall Bridge, which crosses the Shropshire Union canal.

2 Turn right over the canal bridge onto a peaceful lane, still on the Staffordshire Way. Walk on this hedged lane, passing to the left of Woolley Farm. Bear right at the next junction, towards Hyde Farm. In about 100 yards, turn left and continue along the Way into an avenue of trees called Upper Avenue.

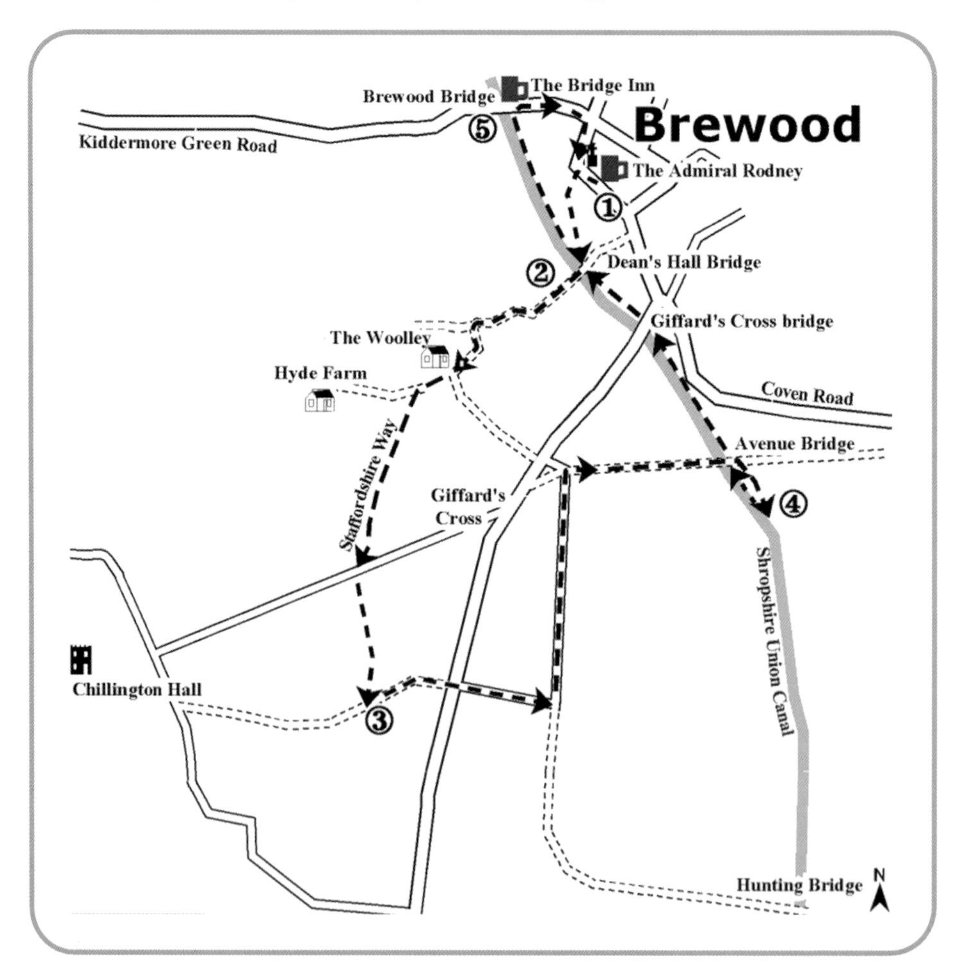

About half a mile to your right is Chillington Hall, the home of the Giffard family since the 12th century. The superb park is a favourite place for local walkers and is open all year.

Continue along the Staffordshire Way over the next field until you reach a lane.

Speedwell Castle

3 Turn left and go along this quiet country lane, crossing over the junction. In about 400 yards, the lane bends sharp left and you follow this (Park Lane) back to the avenue of trees; here turn right and descend tree-lined Lower Avenue. In about 600 yards, you will reach Avenue Bridge over the canal, where you drop down to the towpath. (Head left for a short distance to enjoy the reflection of the unusual bridge balustrade in the waters of the canal.)

4 Now go beneath Avenue Bridge and walk along the canal towpath. Pass beneath Giffard's Cross Bridge and then Dean's Hall Bridge. (From here there is a good view over the village of Brewood.) Continue beneath School Bridge to arrive at Brewood Bridge.

5 Leave the towpath, going right through a white gate, to arrive on the roadside in Brewood opposite the Bridge Inn. Turn right and go along the pavement in High Green into the centre of Brewood, entering the village through Bargate Street and then bearing right into Market Place. (Do take your time to explore the history of Brewood's many fine buildings.) Turn right into Church Road; then bear left through the churchyard of St Mary and St Chad to find the grave of Colonel William Careless, a soldier, who, after the battle of Worcester in 1651, hid King Charles II in the Royal Oak at nearby Boscobel House. Leave the churchyard through a gate into Dean Street. Then turn left, passing yet more 18th-century buildings, to return to the Admiral Rodney.

Date walk completed:

....

Place of Interest

Chillington Hall has been the home of the Giffards since 1178. It is a beautiful place to visit, with its park and lake landscaped by 'Capability' Brown. It was described in 1767 as having 'confessedly one of the finest pieces of water, within an inclosure, that this Kingdom produces'. Telephone: 01902 850236.

Walk 20 Wombourne

The Plough Inn

This easy walk is along a disused railway track and the towpath of the historic Staffordshire and Worcestershire canal, where there are many colourful narrowboats to admire. At Bratch Locks you can enjoy one of the finest treasures along the canal: the amazing 30 ft 2 in. locks. From the top there is a clear view down the valley, with the spire of Wombourne church against the backdrop of the Orton Hills. Three lock gates set very close together by an attractive octagonal toll house combine to form a picture-postcard sight, much photographed by the many visitors in summer.

Distance: *7½ miles*

OS Explorer 219
GR 867937

An undemanding, level walk

Starting point: The Bratch Locks car park.

How to get there: The Bratch Locks car park is to the west of Wolverhampton, just off the A449 road.

The **Plough Inn** on School Road, Trysull, guarantees a friendly welcome and good home-made food for walkers who visit the lounge or the large garden of this 300-year-old pub. Dishes can include gammon steak and Cajun chicken, as well as snacks such as jacket potatoes and hot roast baguettes.

Opening times *are from 11.30 am to 3 pm, Monday to Friday, and all day from 11.30 am at weekends. During the week food is available from 12 noon to 2.30 pm and from 6 pm to 8.30 pm, and between 12 noon and 4 pm at the weekend; there are no evening meals on Sunday.*

Telephone: *01902 892254.*

The Walk

1 Descend from the back of the small car park at the Bratch picnic area onto the towpath of the Staffordshire and Worcestershire canal, and head south. After about 220 yards, turn left over a stile into pastureland; then bear left again, following the hedge-line up to a stile hidden behind bushes. Go over the stile, bearing left up a hedged footpath. At the end, turn right, and then left behind houses; walk on towards a bridge over the Kingswinford Railway Walk. Turn left just before you reach the bridge and go on the footpath that leads down to the walkway. As you walk along this for the next 2¼ miles, you pass several picnic tables and go beneath a number of road bridges.

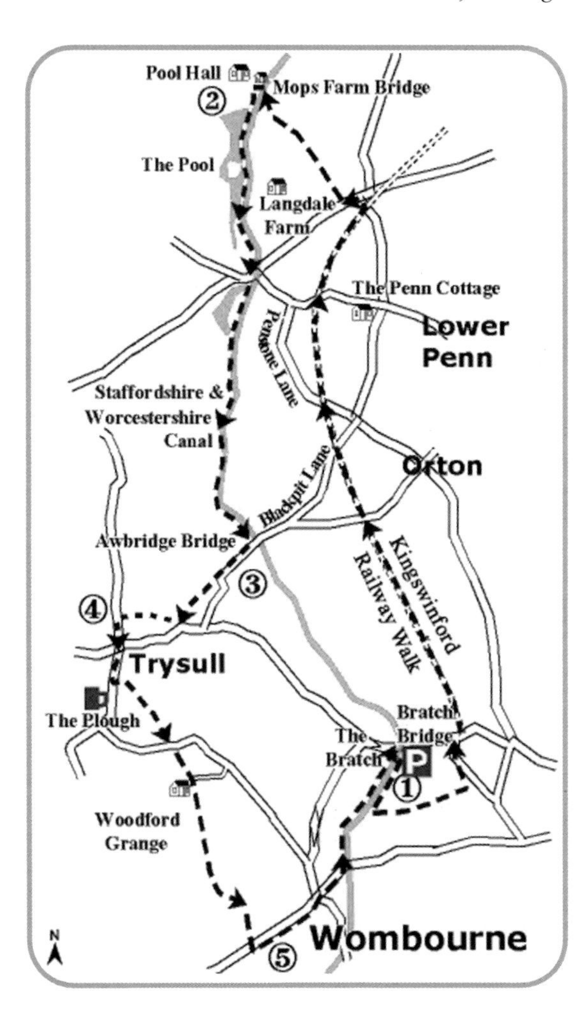

Immediately after walking beneath the Langley Road bridge, go left and ascend steps up to the road. Go left along the road, and then turn right over a stile into a cultivated field. Walk on the public footpath to the right of the field hedge beneath electricity wires. At the field end, bear left and walk on the other side of the hedge over the next field. The path bends left and then right to emerge on a lane next to Pool Hall Cottages and Mops Farm Bridge.

2 Turn left over the bridge. Then, in about 100 yards, turn left through a gate into pastureland. Walk on the farm track to a second gate for horses, passing to the left of an attractive stretch of water known as The Pool. Walk on this clear path for about half a mile, with the pool to your right and the Staffordshire and Worcestershire canal to your left. Pass through the gate onto a path, passing some rather dilapidated buildings. After walking along the towpath for about 1½ miles you reach

Awbridge Bridge (no. 49) and climb up to a quiet country road.

❸ Turn right over the bridge and go up the road towards Trysull, passing Orchard Cottage on the way. At the road bend, keep ahead and cross a cultivated field, passing beneath electric power lines. At the field end, turn right over the stile in the hedge and continue along the footpath that passes below a flower-laden cottage. Cross a bridge over the stream to reach the road at the edge of Trysull village.

❹ Head left along the road (Trysull Holloway), passing Thatcher's Cottage to reach Bell Road. Go right along the road for about 25 yards; then go left up School Road into the centre of the village. After passing by All Saints' church, you will soon reach the Plough Inn.

From the inn retrace your steps towards the village, but go right along a waymarked hedged footpath. After going through a hand-gate, aim for Woodford Cottage, set in the far right-hand corner of the field, and pass through a hedge gap onto Woodford Lane. Here, turn left, and, in about 25 yards, go right down the driveway to Woodford Grange. Cross over the stream and you will soon arrive near the grange building. Walk along the public footpath to the left of the buildings and then, after passing some dilapidated vehicles, bear right. Continue along the clear footpath, with a row of electricity pylons over to your left; a field stile leads onto a wide track, which soon becomes a disused tarmac road. After passing a couple of large boulders blocking access, you will arrive at Poolhouse Road, the Bridgnorth road.

Narrowboats near Bratch bridge

❺ Cross the road with care, pass through the gap in the hedge, and go left for about 400 yards, onto a quiet footpath set inside the roadside hedge of The Meadlands residential estate. When you reach the pavement of Poolhouse Road, go past the massive Ferro factory. At bridge no. 43 on the Staffordshire and Worcestershire canal, join the towpath and head left towards Wombourne. You pass Bumble Hole lock, and will soon see Bratch Common to your left, with its abundance of wildflowers (it was once a small lake). Continue along the towpath to the Bratch lock car park.

Place of Interest
Wightwick Manor (National Trust), 4 miles to the north, in Wolverhampton, is a superb Victorian manor house, with William Morris interior decoration and a colourful 17-acre garden. Telephone: 01902 761400.

Date walk completed:

....

Barlaston

The Duke of York

A walk full of interest, it starts from the attractive village of Barlaston and embraces a delightful stroll along the towpath of the Trent and Mersey canal. There is the opportunity to visit the famous Wedgwood factory – perhaps take a tour – and on the return route you will pass Barlaston Hall, a beautiful Georgian mansion, and perhaps make time to admire the many attractive houses in the village.

***Distance:** 3½ miles*

OS Explorer 258
GR 894384

An easy, short walk

Starting point: The car park of the Duke of York pub in Barlaston.

How to get there: Barlaston is 6 miles south of Stoke-on-Trent. Leave Stoke-on-Trent on the A34 road. In 5 miles turn left onto the Tittensor road, signed to Barlaston. The Duke of York is in Longton Road in the middle of the village.

The **Duke of York**, a 200-year-old pub, was once a frontage for four cottages. Today, it is a well-established hostelry that offers good wholesome bar snacks from home-made soup to sandwiches, baps, baguettes and jacket potatoes. You can also eat your own sandwiches in the garden, provided that you buy a drink from the inn.

***Opening times** are from 11 am to 4.30 pm and from 6 pm to 11 pm, Monday to Thursday; all day from 11 am on Friday and Saturday; and from 11 am to 5 pm on Sundays. Food is available between 12 noon and 2.30 pm every day of the week.*

Telephone: 01782 374221.

The Walk

❶ From the car park at the Duke of York go to the road and head left towards the large village green and Station Road. Turn right at the main road and pass the village library, an attractive building that in 1680 was a school. About 150 yards further on, cross the road and turn left onto a clear track set to the right of the modern parish church of St John the Baptist. The track is sited on the left side of the hedge and goes generally south-westwards over pastureland. Soon it switches to the right of the hedge and becomes a footpath. After about half a mile of easy, pleasant walking, turn left, and go over a stile in the hedge onto a track. Turn right and walk below the railway bridge; cross the bridge over the Trent and Mersey canal; and then go down to its towpath.

❷ Turn left (northwards) beneath the bridge and follow the towpath; soon you will pass along the rear of some attractive private gardens, which are a mass of flowers in spring and summer. After going beneath the bridge by the Plume and Feather Inn, continue along the towpath and take in the very peaceful scene (interrupted occasionally by an inter-city train speeding along the railway line that runs parallel with the canal). As you approach bridge no. 104 (Old Road Bridge), you will soon see the massive Wedgwood factory on the far right bank of the canal. (It is easy to imagine the horse-drawn barges of old making their way along the canal into Birmingham with their load of Wedgwood pottery. What an impressive sight that must have been.)

❸ Climb up to the road at bridge 104, cross over it, and walk up the lane to visit the Wedgwood factory, passing to the left of Wedgwood station.

The Wedgwood Group is the largest china and earthenware manufacturer in the world, and Barlaston factory, with its six 'clean' electric tunnel ovens, is at the centre of the industry. Until Josiah Wedgwood built this new factory, which started production in 1940 at the start of the Second World War, Barlaston would have been a sleepy village. This peaceful picture changed when the railway and the Trent and Mersey Canal took over the transportation for the famous pottery.

After your visit to the factory, return to the road and head left up the quiet road to continue your walk.

❹ In about 200 yards, turn right into Queen Mary's Drive and from there go into Barlaston. Along the way you will pass the impressive building of Barlaston Hall.

Elegant Barlaston Hall

In 1773 a picture of the hall appeared on a dinner service made for the Empress Catherine of Russia. During the Second World War, Barlaston Hall became the headquarters of the Bank of England. Today, it is privately owned and it is not open to the public; so please respect the privacy of the owners.

Continue along the drive and go down Longton Road into Barlaston village. You will pass several very attractive houses, and soon find The Duke of York public house, on your left.

Place of Interest

The Wedgwood Visitor Centre, Barlaston is on the route of the walk route. It houses an award-winning 'living' museum, together with craft demonstrations by potters and decorators. Exhibitions are mounted throughout the year. Telephone: 01782 204218.

Date walk completed:

....

Walk 22 Cannock Chase

The Barley Mow

Cannock Chase is an area of countryside which has eternal appeal for the walker. While offering a scenic landscape, it does not include major hills to deter the everyday walker. This attractive walk starts from Milford Common and quickly reaches the towpath of the Staffordshire and Worcester canal, passing the many colourful narrowboats that congregate in the area during the summer months. Shugborough Hall can be seen through the trees, and you will pass by some very attractive large houses on the outskirts of Great Haywood before entering the chase for the final stretch of the walk back to the common, at the end of a most enjoyable mix of scenery.

Although the **Barley Mow** (a Mitchells and Butlers retail outlet) has modernized extensively over recent years in an attempt to attract the younger person, it has, nevertheless, retained an appeal for the very many walkers on Cannock Chase. Good quality food and good beer always stand well, and you can be sure of these when you visit the Barley Mow. Perhaps you will be tempted by the peppered mushrooms and the 'Surf and Turf', a 6 oz steak cooked with golden fried tempura shrimps.

Opening times *are from 11 am to 11 pm (10.30 pm on Sunday) every day of the week. Food is available between 12 noon and 9 pm during the week, and up to 10 pm on Saturday and 8 pm on Sunday.*

Telephone: *01785 665293.*

Distance: *7 miles*

OS Explorer 244
GR 973210

An easy walk along a towpath and good tracks

Starting point: Milford Common car park

How to get there: Milford is just over 4 miles from Stafford. From Stafford take the A34 and in about 2 miles continue on the A513, which leads to Milford.

The Walk

1 From the car park cross the A513 road, and go down the Tixall road which is sited to the left of the entrance gates to Shugborough Hall. Go over the railway bridge and the river Sow to reach the Tixall Bridge over the Staffordshire and Worcestershire canal. Go down to the canal towpath and head east, walking on the right bank of the canal. Pass Tixall lock and go under Oldhill Bridge (no. 107) before reaching the Tixall Wide, a 275m stretch of the canal which was deliberately widened to form a sort of lake to former Tixall Hall. (Here you can expect moored narrowboats to add to a perfect scene.) Continue beneath the swivel bridge. After passing the aqueduct, you will see a number of colourful narrowboats near the repair facilities at the Great Haywood Junction. Go under the elegant sweeping arch bridge at Great Haywood junction, a bridge made famous by the photography of canal historian Eric de Maré.

2 Now turn right onto the towpath of the Trent and Mersey canal and continue along it, going generally south eastwards. You will pass Lockhouse Restaurant on the far bank and go beneath bridge 73

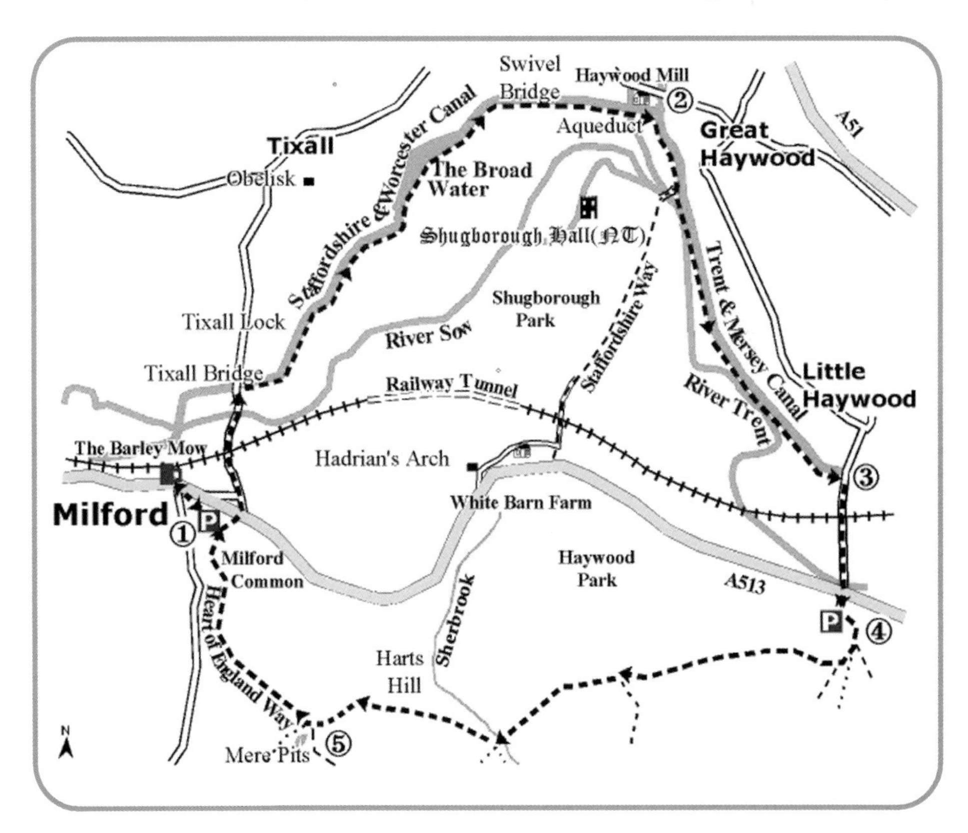

(from here you can reach the village of Great Haywood). Continue along the towpath for a further mile. At first you will have the river Trent to your right, and you should get a good view of Shugborough Hall. The canal is to your left, and beyond this you will see the lovely houses in Great Haywood.

❸ At bridge no. 72, leave the towpath by climbing some steps and turn right along a country road. Go beneath the railway bridge and cross the A513 road.

❹ Now go along the track ahead onto Cannock Chase. Soon you reach the Seven Springs car park and picnic area. Here, turn right and go past the forestry barrier; in a few yards, take the right-hand fork (the broader track) at a junction of paths and tracks. Bear right again at the next junction. Soon the undulating track will take you through a mix of broadleaf woodland and conifer plantations. As you progress, the track will take you into the Sherbrook valley at the stepping stones, a very attractive place where the scattered trees mix pleasingly with grassy glades surrounded by wooded and heather-covered slopes. Cross the stepping stones; in a few yards you will reach a junction of tracks, where you bear right to walk through the trees of Brocton Coppice. After about 650 yards of lovely easy walking you will reach a junction of tracks. Turn left, soon to arrive near Mere Pits.

Walkers on the Heart of England Way

❺ Turn right and join the Heart of England Way. Follow the distinctive waymarkers back to Milford Common, walking at first in a north-westerly direction. In about 550 yards, turn right at the crossway, and shortly go left to complete the final stretch of the Heart of England Way on a path which descends to the car park.

Date walk completed:

....

Place of Interest

Shugborough Hall (National Trust) is the home of Lord Lichfield, the famous photographer. It was built in 1693 and later enlarged by Thomas Anson. The wings were added about 1750, and then in 1794 the eight-columned portico was built to complete the superb façade. Inside, there is rich decoration with fine rococo plasterwork, and there are interesting collections of 18th-century ceramics, silverware, paintings and French furniture. If you enter the property through the gateway to Shugborough Farm Museum, you will see the Arch of Hadrian on the left, which was built in 1761 to celebrate Anson's circumnavigation of the world in 1740–44. A copy of Hadrian's Arch in Athens, it stands on the site of the original village of Shugborough and contains the busts of Admiral Lord Anson and his wife. Telephone: 01889 881388.

Meerbrook 23 Walk

The Lazy Trout

A walk onto The Roaches is a dream, for there are so many wonderful views to enjoy. Our route starts from the village of Meerbrook and climbs gently over farmland up to the famous rocks. As you walk past the trig point it is hard to believe that you are only at 550m, for the panorama is exceptional. Pick a good weather day for this walk and take your time to enjoy the atmosphere before you return over pastureland to the Lazy Trout.

Distance: *7½ miles*

OS Outdoor Leisure 24
GR 990607

A hill walk

Starting point: The Lazy Trout in Meerbrook

How to get there: Meerbrook is 4½ miles north of Leek. Leave Leek on the A53, and in about 3 miles turn left down local roads to reach Meerbrook.

Many years ago, **The Lazy Trout** was known as The Three Horseshoes, but it was frequently confused with a pub of the same name on the A53. Because the pub obtains its supply of fresh table trout from nearby Tittesworth reservoir, it was renamed The Lazy Trout. It is a pleasure to sit out in the garden and look up at the impressive Roaches. You can select from sandwiches to a variety of main courses, but the locally-caught trout is no doubt the favourite of many.

Opening times *are from 12 noon until 11 pm each day of the week. Food is available from 12 noon to 2.30 pm and from 6 pm to 9 pm.*

Telephone: *01538 300385*

The Walk

1 Leave the car park at the Lazy Trout and turn right. Go past the inn, and turn right past the YHA hostel. Continue up the road for about 35 yards (the church is set back to the left); then turn right again. Stroll up a driveway, passing a couple of country cottages, and follow the waymarkers for the Staffordshire Moorlands Walk as you enter the Peak National Park. At the end of the cottages, cross over a couple of stiles and walk on the footpath that hugs the left-hand hedge. After passing through a farm gate and going over a further stile, bear right and walk on a stone track towards the farm called Frith Bottom. Just before reaching the farm, turn right and go over a stile onto a raised boarded area above a rather wet patch. After going over a second stile, you will arrive in pastureland. Aim for a mid-field marker post and head left here, passing to the right of Frith Bottom and continuing to the right of the hedge up to a stile in the

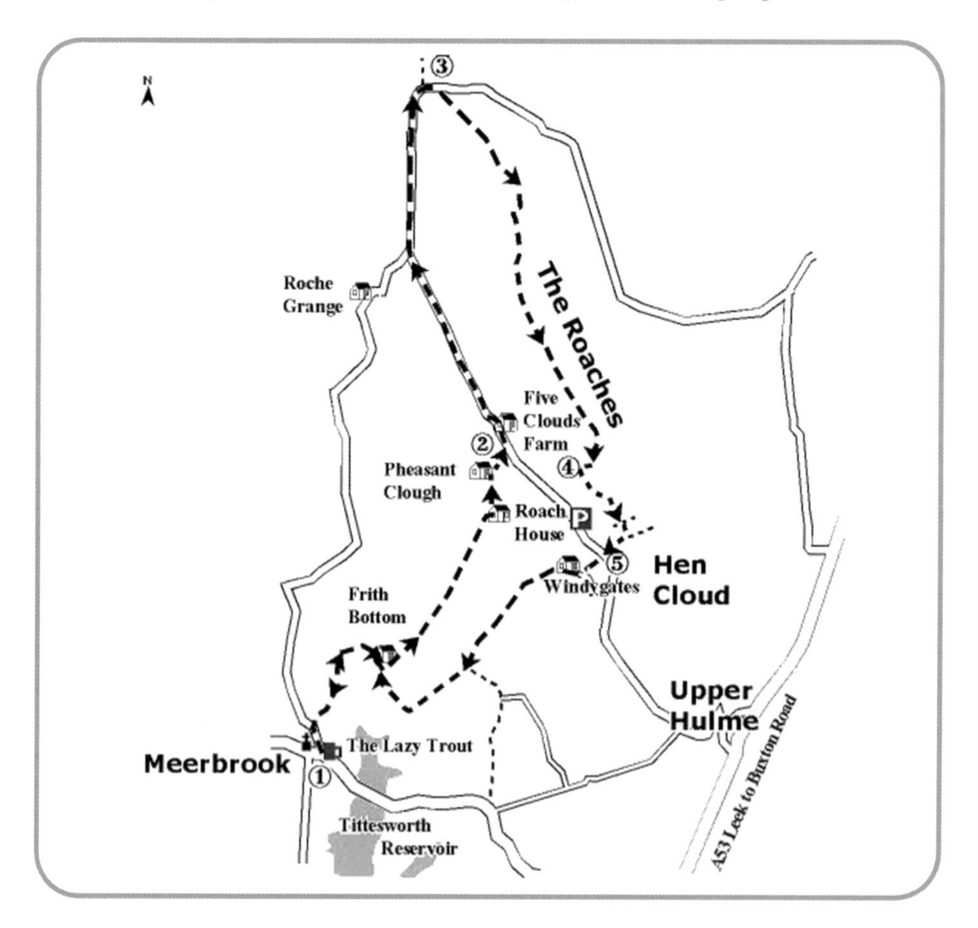

top left-hand corner of the field. Go over the stile, walking to the right of the hedge, and, at the end of the second field, switch to the left-hand side of the hedge on the approach to Roach House. Pass to the left of the house, and continue over a couple of stiles to arrive at the farm complex of Pheasants Clough. Walk between the farm buildings, following the waymarker direction. After going through a farm gate set to the left of the farmhouse, follow the waymarker direction, going over another stile and then heading up the field to a farm gate onto a quiet road, almost opposite to Five Clouds Farm, which is situated below The Roaches.

❷ Turn left and walk along the gated road for about 1½ miles.

❸ After passing through a third gate, bear right and climb up a footpath over the top of The Roaches. Now you can enjoy a superlative stretch of hill walking, with stunning views all round. Initially, the footpath over the hill is built of stone slabs; it then becomes a stony/sandy surface that makes for easy walking as you progress past a series of rocky areas. Look out for rock climbers, who can regularly be seen attempting to climb the rockface. Just before reaching the end of the main hill chain, turn right at a timber rail and descend from the hilltop down a stony path.

❹ At the waymarker post, turn left, and walk on the clear footpath below the hilltop. Continue down the path until you reach a hand gate in a stone wall. Go through the gate and aim for a hand gate in the next stone wall; turn right in front of it and walk down the footpath to the road.

The Roaches

❺ Cross the road and go over the stile opposite, into pastureland, walking to the left of the hedge as you go towards Windygates Farm. Turn right along the farm drive, and bear left to go over a stile set to the right of a barn. At the end of the barn, bear left and follow the waymarker going left. Maintain this direction over a couple of large fields until you reach a stone stile by a farm gate. Go over the stile, and follow the Staffordshire Moorlands Walk waymarkers to a stile set to the right of an old barn. Continue to a further stile; then turn right. A pair of stiles will take you back to the raised boards and stone track near Frith Bottom. Retrace your steps to the Lazy Trout Inn.

Place of Interest

Tittesworth Reservoir, half a mile south-east, is in the Peak National Park and offers a relaxing day out for the family. There is a large visitor centre and plenty of opportunities for bird spotting. Telephone: 01538 300400.

Date walk completed:

....

Walk 24

Abbots Bromley

The Goat's Head

A chance to visit the ancient town of Abbots Bromley, recorded in the Domesday Book as Brunlege. One of the earliest landowners was the Bagot family (ancestors of the Earls of Stafford); the walk takes you along a road named after them. The town is most famous for the Abbots Bromley horn dance, one of the oldest ritual dances still performed in England, which takes place in early September. Originally, it was held to commemorate the acquisition by the villagers of Abbots Bromley of hunting rights in the nearby Needwood Forest. The dance consists of six men carrying sets of reindeer horns who, accompanied by the traditional folk fool, the man-woman, hobby horse and boy hunter, symbolically process through the village, neighbouring villages and outlying farms, 'bringing in the luck'. At 7.45 am they turn up to collect the horns (which are over 1,000 years old) from St Nicholas' church, a singular occasion, indeed.

Distance: *3 miles*

OS Explorer 244
GR 080245

An easy walk

Starting point: The Goat's Head in Abbots Bromley

How to get there: Abbots Bromley is 7 miles south of Uttoxeter. Leave Uttoxeter on the A518. In about a mile, turn left onto the B5013 to arrive in the town.

The black and white half-timbered **Goat's Head** in Market Place is a landmark in the town. It dates from the 16th century and contains a room named after Dick Turpin, who is reputed to have stayed a night there. You can be assured of a good meal at the inn, for the meat, supplied by local butchers and sourced from Staffordshire farms, is always fresh. The landlord offers a wide selection of food, from sandwiches to bass fillet with tangy lemon sauce, as well as special Dutch meals. Sunday lunch can be very special. Perhaps you will decide to enjoy your meal in the beautiful garden at the rear of the inn. Greene King Abbot and Marston's Pedigree are on tap, and the service is friendly and efficient.

Opening times *are between 12 noon and 3 pm and from 6 pm to 11 pm during the week; and from 12 noon to 4 pm and from 7 pm to 10.30 pm on Sunday. Food is available every day of the week.*

Telephone: *01283 840254.*

The Walk

1 Leave Market Place in Abbots Bromley by walking up School Road (opposite the Goat's Head Inn) and you will soon pass Mr Clarke's First School. Follow the Staffordshire waymarker, and then turn right along Swan Lane. At the end of Swan Lane, leave the way and turn right onto a footpath that leads you past

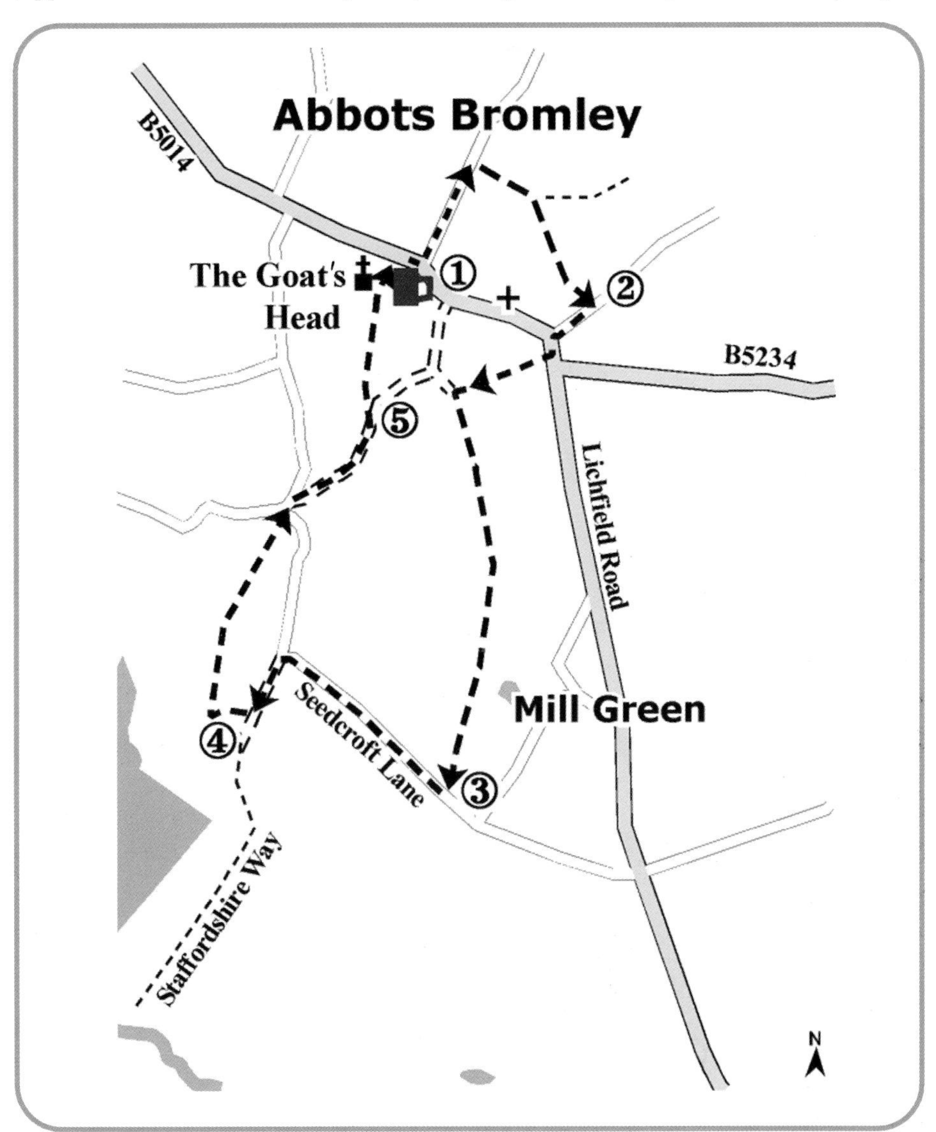

the back of the school of St Mary and St Anne to reach Radmore Lane.

The market place, Abbots Bromley

❷ Turn right and walk down the lane into the town and arrive on a corner of High Street. Turn left, and walk down High Street for about 50 yards; then cross over the street and head down a driveway by a bus stop and milepost. In about 250 yards, the driveway bends right, and here you bear left, walking along the edge of playing fields. Leave through the gap in the fence and continue to the left of the field edge, skirting the school playing fields. Cross over the boundary fence and continue along the field edge. You will see Mill Green Farm to the left and will soon pass some oak trees and a small pond to reach the field corner, where you go onto Seedcroft Lane.

❸ Turn right and walk along the lane, passing by Seedcroft Farm and some detached houses, to arrive at a bend in the road. Turn left and go down Waters Road, following the signpost to Blithfield reservoir and a sailing club.

❹ In about 200 yards, turn right and re-join the Staffordshire Way, heading towards the field gateway. Go right over a stile immediately before the gateway, and walk on the tree-lined avenue going generally north-eastwards. At the field edge continue along the boundary until you reach a stile in the corner. Continue to follow the waymarkers of the Staffordshire Way all of the way back into Abbots Bromley. Soon you reach Seedcroft Lane once again. Here turn left into Goose Lane; then bear right into Hall Hill Lane. Follow this lane towards the town.

❺ In about 250 yards, turn left, go over a stile and follow the waymarker direction up the right-hand side of the field towards the church ahead. After passing the entrance to Severn Trent sewage treatment works, follow a grassy track up to a stile on the left; then continue along the way and to arrive in the churchyard. Pass to the right of the church to reach the lychgate into Bagot Street. Turn right along Bagot Street to reach the Goat's Head on the corner of Market Place.

Place of Interest
Sudbury Hall (National Trust), 7 miles away, is a late 17th-century house with sumptuous interiors. Telephone: 01283 585337; 01283 585305 (info line).

Date walk completed:

....

Dimmingsdale

The Ramblers Retreat

This is a fine walk into the beautiful woodland around Dimmingsdale. The route takes you into the Forestry Commission dreamland of magnificent drives built by the Earl of Shrewsbury a true beauty spot. You will stroll past trout pools and ascend onto a lane from where you will enjoy a superb view of the world famous Alton Towers (once owned by the Earls of Shrewsbury). A steep descent leads to the edge of Oakamoor before you stroll along a dismantled railway line back to the Ramblers Retreat.

The **Ramblers Retreat.** Although not strictly speaking a pub it would be remiss of me not to include the Ramblers Retreat in this book. It is a family run restaurant and coffee house which is well known among the rambling fraternity. Formerly Dimmingsdale Lodge on the Earl of Shrewsbury's estate it was used for residential purposes until the 1960s. Having been left unoccupied for many years a dereliction order was placed on the building in 1978. At that time Gary and Margaret Keeling purchased the building and restored it. The lounge was opened in 1981 to sell tea and scones and it has now become a favourite haunt of ramblers across Staffordshire and Derbyshire. There is a full menu of delicious food available offering snack lunches and full meals to suit taste and time available. The meringue pie is rather special. You can rely upon a wonderful experience at the Ramblers Retreat which is open every day of the year except on Christmas Day.

Opening times *for food are from 10 am to 6 pm in summer and from 10 am to 5 pm during the winter months. Alcoholic drinks are served with meals but tea and coffee are available at any time.*

Telephone: *01538 702730.*

Distance: *4½ miles*

OS Explorer 259
GR: 062431

A superb walk into Dimmingsdale and along a dismantled railway track for refreshments at the wonderful Ramblers Retreat

Starting point: Dimmingsdale car park near to the Ramblers Retreat

How to get there: Oakamoor is 13 miles north of Uttoxeter. Take the A50 road from Uttoxeter and in 2.4 miles bear right onto the A522 towards Cheadle. In Cheadle turn right onto the B5417 road. Turn right just before reaching Oakamoor and drive down Red Lane to the Dimmingsdale car park.

The Walk

1 From the Dimmingsdale car park ascend onto the Staffordshire Way going left (south east). Walk the clear wide waymarked footpath into the trees of Threap Wood for some 150 yards and then turn sharp right up a footpath that ascends around the side of the hill. This is lovely woodland walking as you progress in a generally westerly direction. In about 250 yards you will pass to the left of a couple of cottages (one derelict and burnt out) and soon go over a stile onto open land with a stone wall to your right. Continue ahead along the clear footpath over undulating grassland. All too soon the path descends to a stile into the trees of Dimmingsdale. The footpath now descends rather steeply and you will cross over a footbridge before continuing in a north-westerly direction. As you progress along the good wide footpath you will be walking by a stream that soon widens to become a small lake. After walking by the side of this for about 200 yards you will reach a crossing with a selection of way-markers to consider. Continue ahead to the right of the lakes maintaining your north-westerly direction. Walk this good wide footpath along the banks of the waterways and in about three quarters of a mile you will arrive at a road junction in the hamlet of Oldfurnace.

2 Turn right at the road and walk along the side of it for the next 400 yards until you reach a junction of lanes. Here, turn right and stroll along the quiet lane that

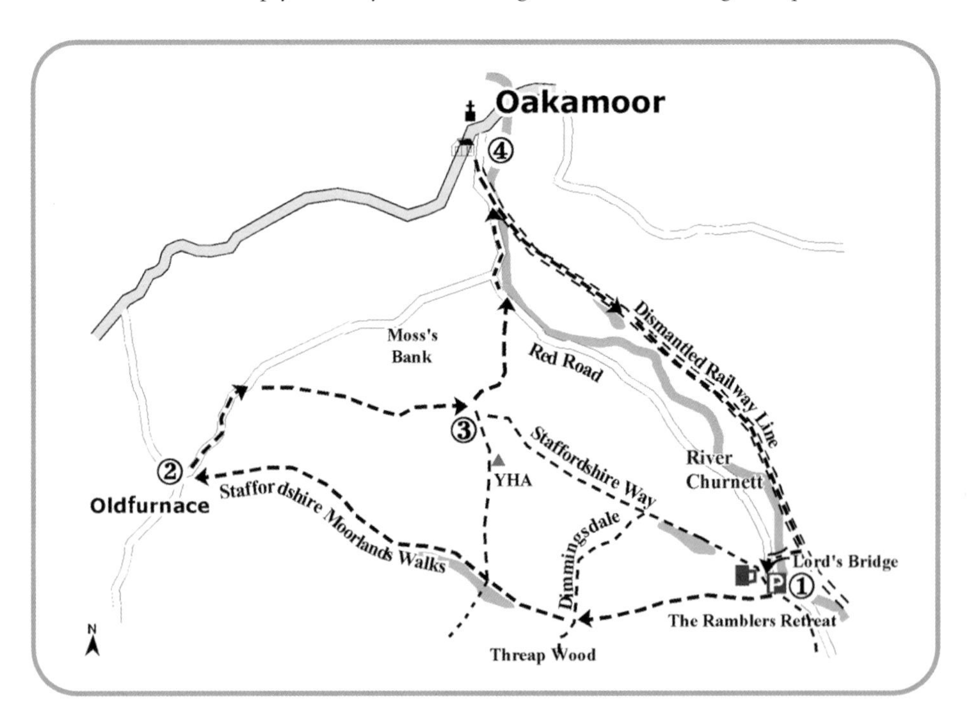

The fine woodland around Dimmingsdale

hugs the top of the hill and offers pleasing views as you progress. After walking the lane for about half a mile you may get a glimpse of the castle building at Alton Towers on the horizon. Soon you will see a country cottage to your left.

3 Here bear left and follow the yellow waymarker direction that leads onto a stone-lined footpath that leads towards the left-hand side of the cottage. Just before reaching the cottage boundary, turn left and pass through a hand-gate into the trees on Moss's Bank. Descend the clear footpath down through the trees (a rather steep descent through the woodland) and eventually you will arrive on Red Road at the bottom of the trees. Turn left and walk along the road for about 125 yards to a road junction. Turn right and walk on the side of the narrow quiet road until you reach an attractive former railway building.

4 Here, turn right and proceed along the dismantled railway line walking in a south-easterly direction. This is very easy walking along a good track. Soon you will pass the remains of the former railway station and then to your right you will see sporting fields down below you. After walking this easy track for about a mile you will arrive by Lord's Bridge. Ascend up to and cross over the bridge and then proceed over a river bridge to arrive by the Ramblers Retreat and the car park where you started the walk.

Place of Interest
Alton Towers (1 mile east) offers a theme park day out for the family with fine gardens to enjoy. Telephone: 01538 702200. Website www.alton-towers.co.uk

Date walk completed:

....

Walk 26 Ellastone

The Duncombe Arms

After visiting St Peter's church (the resting place of over 40 Finneys) in Upper Ellastone, this pretty walk takes you into attractive parkland and past the ruins of Calwich Abbey. Soon you are walking along the side of the river Dove into the ancient village of Middle Mayfield - part of the village of Mayfield which predates the Domesday Book, where it is called *Mavreveldt.* The route then takes you onto the hills nearby and you return to Ellastone along the Limestone Way passing back through the St Peter's churchyard.

Distance: *6 miles*

OS Explorer 259
GR 116434

An easy walk into typical Staffordshire countryside. You will pass by an old abbey and walk by the side of the river Dove before returning along a stretch of the Limestone Way.

Starting point: The village car park in Ellastone situated off Church Road.

How to get there: Ellastone is 3 miles north of Rocester. Leave Rocester on the B5030 road and in about 2½ miles bear right onto the B5032 road to reach Ellastone.

The 17th-century **Duncombe Arms** is named after Sir Charles Duncombe, the Lord of the Manor. It was originally a coaching inn on the Ashbourne to Uttoxeter road and has an excellent garden overlooking Calwich Abbey.

Opening times *are Thursday to Saturday 12 noon to 3 pm and from 6 pm to 11 pm plus all day on Sunday. It is closed at lunchtime on Monday, Tuesday and Wednesday but otherwise food is available throughout opening hours.*

Telephone: *01335 324242.*

The Walk

1 Exit the car park and turn right then immediately left into the churchyard of St Peter's, Ellastone. Pass to the right of the church and exit via a kissing gate at the rear of the churchyard. Descend the field to a stile by a gate to arrive on the B5032. Head left along the edge of the road for about 100 yards going over a bridge over Titbrook. Turn right just after passing a lodge building and walk to its left through a gateway onto a footpath that initially arcs right and then left through farm gates. Stroll along the wide stone track through the attractive Calwich Park. After about 600 yards enter the trees and pass to the left of the ruins of Calwich Abbey. Continue along the track which becomes a tarmac lane. To your right look out for a green-roofed temple to Music and Art by the lake. This is where Handel is said to have composed his famous Water Music. You pass to the right of Calwich Home Farm.

2 Turn right onto a stone farm track that arcs right towards a house called The Grove. Before reaching the private dwelling bear left away from its driveway onto a grass track that continues to arc right. Bear left aiming for a stile in the field hedge and go over the footbridge into pastureland aiming for Toadhole Foot Bridge over the river Dove. If you go over the bridge you will be in Derbyshire so stay on the Staffordshire side of the river. Now turn sharp left aiming for a stile in the field hedge about 25 yards away from the Dove. Do not follow the main route towards the trees of Cockley Wood but turn right and take the footpath along the edge of the Dove. The Dove bends right away from the footpath and then arcs back towards a junction of footpaths. Here bear left and proceed up

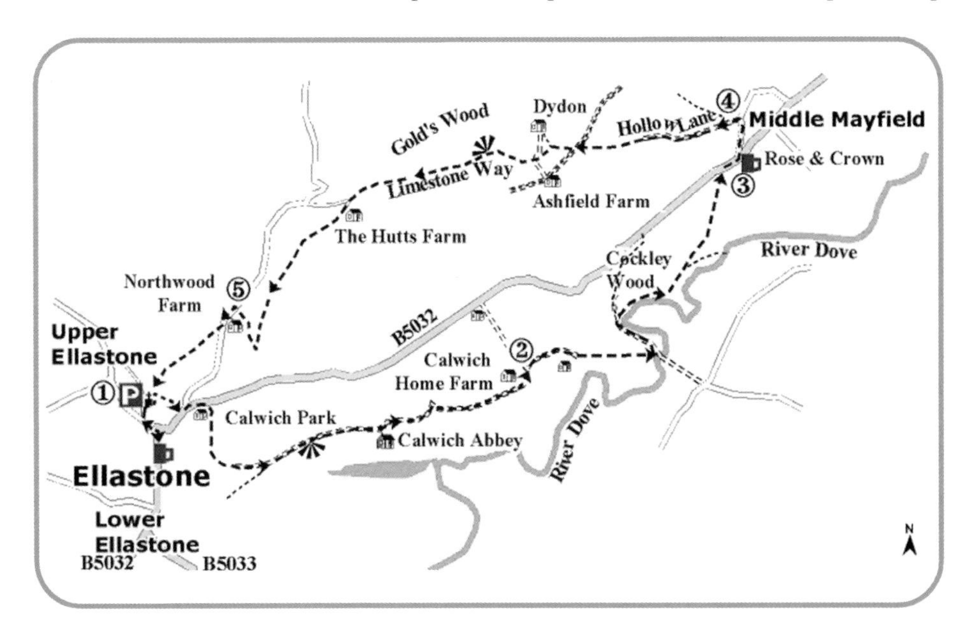

towards the village of Middle Mayfield on a green path aiming towards a stile by a farm gate onto the B5030. Turn right and stroll into the village.

3 When near to the Rose and Crown pub, cross over the road and proceed up Hermitage Lane opposite. In about 200 yards you will reach a stand for milk churns by Hollow Lane.

4 Head left up Hollow Lane. The hedged lane becomes an earth footway ascending away from the village. After passing by a cottage, go over stiles and continue up the rather steep footpath to its top and into pastureland. Follow the waymarker directions and walk ahead. You will go over a series of stiles and join the Limestone Way passing to the left of a property called Dydon and to the right of Ashfield Farm - the fine view ahead is of the Weaver Hills. Continue along the Limestone Way going over a series of stiles. After walking to the left of Gold's Wood a stile takes you onto the driveway to The Hutts Farm. Pass to the right of the farm property and continue ahead over a stile by a gate. The woodland continues to your right but is now perhaps 75 yards away from the footpath. Continue ahead following the clear waymarkers and soon you will see Northwood Farm over the stream to your right. Look for and go across a footbridge over the stream and then head up towards the farm. A series of stiles will lead you onto Northwood Lane.

5 Turn left and proceed along the lane for about 100 yards and then bear right over a stile in the hedge. Ahead of you is now a good view over the village of Upper Ellastone and it is a simple matter to follow the waymarker directions over the fields back to the village. Eventually you will arrive back at the hand-gate to re-enter the churchyard. Cross over Church Lane to return to the car park. Stroll down Church Lane and then go right along the B5033 to find the Duncombe Arms public house.

The path leading to St Peter's church

Place of Interest

Norbury Junction (1 mile south-east) is a lovely hamlet situated on the Shropshire Union canal at the junction of what was once the Shrewsbury and Newport canal. You are sure to see a number of colourful narrowboats.

Date walk completed:

....

Grindon 27 Walk

The Cavalier Inn

The tiny village of Grindon is situated on high moorland above the Hamps and Manifold rivers. This interesting walk takes you into the Manifold valley, passing Wetton, where the rivers Hamps and Manifold meet and pursue subterranean channels through the rugged limestone rocks. After passing a lofty and precipitous cliff you will see Thor's House Cavern. There is a lovely stretch of the Manifold Way to enjoy before you climb back to the village along lanes and good tracks.

The **Cavalier Inn** was originally known as the Shoulder of Mutton, prior to which it was the village smithy. It is believed that over 200 years ago it was renamed in honour of Bonnie Prince Charlie, who is reputed to have stayed in the village. The inn is a favourite watering hole with walkers, and, although open only on Friday evenings, weekends and at bank holidays, it is an ideal refreshment stop for anyone wishing to walk in this very attractive but remote area of Staffordshire.

Opening times *are from 7 pm to 11 pm on Friday evening, and from 12 noon until 2.30 pm and from 7 pm to 11 pm (10.30 pm on Sunday) at the weekend. At lunchtime on Saturday and Sunday, food is available from 12 noon until 2 pm.*

Telephone: *01538 304285.*

Distance: *5½ miles*

OS Outdoor Leisure 24
GR 085542

Generally hilly terrain but much of the walk is on good footpaths and tarmac lanes

Starting point: The car park near to All Saints' church in Grindon

How to get there: Grindon is 8 miles south-east of Leek. Approach the village on the A523 Ashbourne road from Leek. In about 6 miles, turn left and follow the road signs into the village.

The Walk

1 From the church car park walk down to the Cavalier Inn.

The church is sometimes referred to as the 'Cathedral of the Moors'. The Rindle Stone, which is situated near the main gate to the church, takes its name from the word rindle *denoting a brook which flows only in wet weather.*

From the inn, cross over the road and walk down the lane opposite, passing Rose Cottage. Then go left, descending towards a row of terraced houses. Before the first house on the right, go right over a stile and walk along the footpath going northwards, descending and then ascending before you go over a stile in a hedge. Aim for the next field corner and go over a stile onto a farm drive. Cross over the driveway and go over the stile opposite; then walk on a bridlepath that descends over stiles/gates into the valley. Shortly after hearing Hoo Brook babbling on your left, go right over a footbridge and continue to Wettonmill. The clear path passes through an attractive valley with Hoo Brook still babbling close to your right. Pass through the mid-valley gate and the waterslacks set in the brook to prevent branches and other debris from drifting downstream – a delightful stretch, with wild flowers as you approach the Manifold Valley. At the valley end, you can cross Wetton Road to visit the mill.

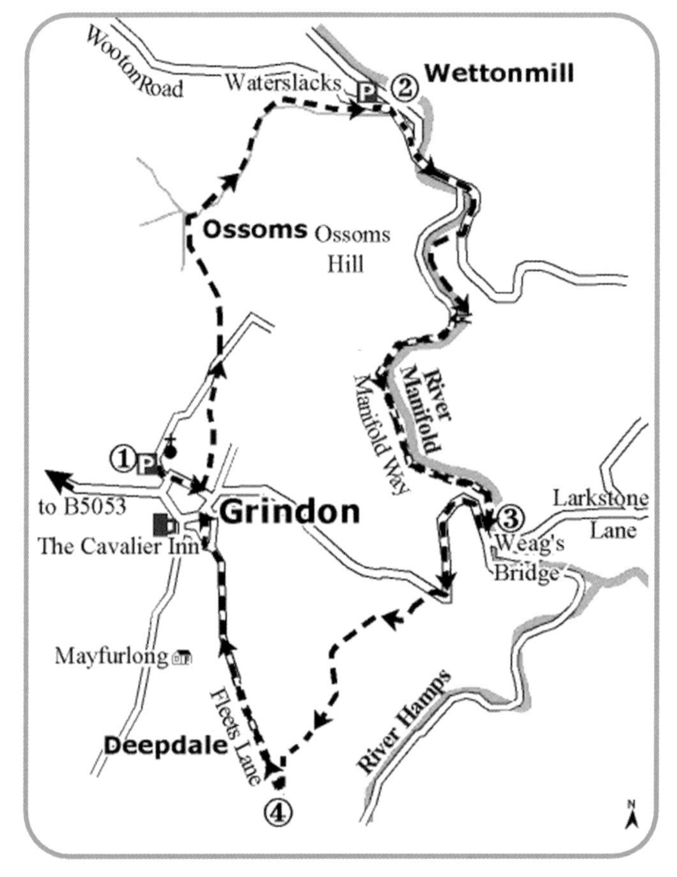

2 Re-cross Wetton Road, and now bear left over the ford in the adjacent lane. This quiet lane by the side of the river Manifold runs parallel to Wetton Road. (However, if the ford is impassable, you may need to walk on Wetton Road, which is quiet but narrow and has passing places for vehicles.) Where the lane meets Wetton Road, turn right and cross the bridge over the river to join the Manifold Way. Continue on the tarmac track that winds its way south by the side of the river. (During summer months the watercourse can dry up, but in winter the water will flow rapidly. For part of its course to Ilam it is an underground river, which appears overground in wet weather.) About three quarters of a mile along the Manifold Way, you will see a footbridge to the right, which you cross to the other side of the river. Thors Cave is in the rocky crag to the left above.

Named after Thor, the Norse god of thunder, the cave has a 40 ft wide mouth, and the dank entrance chamber looks like a Norman arched doorway. There are superb views from here of the surrounding countryside.

3 After an enjoyable stretch of riverside walking, you reach Weag's Bridge. Turn right, and stroll up the quiet road for just under half a mile. Just after the road bends sharp right, go left onto a clear waymarked track, keeping to the right of a stone wall. Go down the track and through a gate, passing to the right of a barn. Continue along the track/bridleway, which curves to the left, still walking to the right of the stone wall as you climb uphill across several fields. (Pause from time to time to enjoy the fine view to the left over the Manifold valley below.) At a field corner the track arcs left again, and in about 120 yards you will reach a junction of paths.

4 Turn sharp right and ascend a farm track/lane (Fleets Lane), at first walking to the right of a stone wall. Maintain your direction up this lane for about half a mile, passing the school to arrive back in Grindon on a lane between dry-stone walls. At the main road in the village, turn left and pass the telephone box and bus shelter to reach the Cavalier Inn.

The church near the start of the walk

Place of Interest

Dovedale (National Trust), 5 miles east, with its famous stepping stones is an idyllic place to visit. Although owned by the National Trust it is freely accessible to the general public.

Date walk completed:

....

Walk 28 *Whittington*

The Swan

This is an easy walk along good footpaths and lanes and the towpath of the historic Coventry canal. In the 18th century the canal was built with the aim of connecting Coventry with a new trade route called the Grand Trunk (the Trent and Mersey canal). The intention was to transport cheap coal from Bedworth coalfield, some 10 miles to the north, and link into a national canal system. The first phase was achieved by 1769, but by the time the canal had reached Atherstone in 1771, all the authorized building capital had been used up, and it took until 1790 for the Coventry canal to finally reach Fradley via a link with the Birmingham and Fazeley canal at the small unpretentious village of Whittington. Because the Coventry Company did not purchase the stretch of canal between Whittington and Fradley, the Coventry bridges tend to be numbered, while the Birmingham and Fazeley bridges are named.

You set out along the towpath, passing the point where the two canals meet, before walking along tracks and footpaths back into the village. A stretch of lane walking provides a good view of the magnificent cathedral city of Lichfield, before you return to the towpath on the way back to Whittington.

Distance: *4¼ miles*

OS Explorer 232
GR 161088

An easy walk along towpaths and quiet country lanes

Starting point: The Swan near the Coventry Canal in Whittington.

How to get there: Whittington is some 4 miles east of Lichfield. Leave Lichfield on the A51 road, and in about 2 miles bear left onto Whittington Common Road to reach the village.

The **Swan** is on the bank of the Coventry canal. There can few better ways of spending a lunch stop than sitting at one of the canal-side benches eating the excellent fare and enjoying a drink. Can you handle a 4-pint pitcher of beer? You can pick from a good menu of bar snacks or you may prefer a meal from the main menu or specials board.

Opening times *are from 12 noon to 3 pm and from 6 pm to 9 pm every day, when both food and drink are available.*

Telephone: *01543 432264.*

The Walk

1 From the Swan car park, turn right to reach the canal bridge and then go down to the towpath of the Coventry canal. Head left (south-eastwards) along the towpath, which at this point runs past the back of some attractive houses. Just after passing bridge no. 78, you come to the commemorative plaque which records the joining of the Coventry canal with the Birmingham and Fazeley Canal; thereafter you will be walking on the towpath of the Birmingham and Fazeley canal until you reach Hademore House Bridge.

2 At the bridge, go from the towpath to the lane; cross over the canal, and follow the footpath going generally south-west over several fields, passing a strawberry field on your left. In about half a mile, you will reach a junction of paths and tracks.

3 Here, turn right onto Vicarage Lane and go into the village of Whittington. You will pass a white cottage. At the end of some playing fields, go right through a hand gate and take the public path to reach Cloister Walk. Turn left and walk along the pavement, past Cloister Lodge and Whittington Old Hall, until you reach a road junction with Whittington Social Club on the corner. Turn right and go past the Dog Inn; walk down Main Street into the village centre.

4 After passing the post office, turn left up Back Lane. In about 150 yards, opposite the end of Blacksmith's Lane, turn right and walk on a hedged footpath

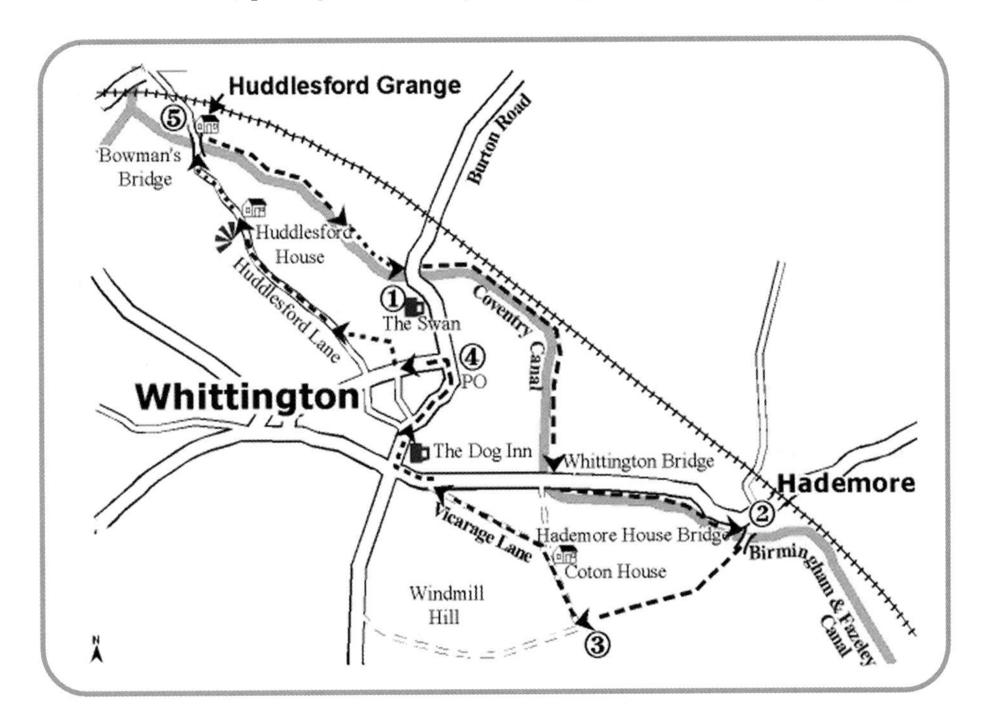

to reach a cultivated field. Cross the field diagonally, aiming for a stile in its far left corner. Cross the stile onto Huddlesford Lane. Now turn right, and head down the quiet lane for the next half a mile, enjoying the peaceful scene and pleasing views. You will pass the very large farm complex of Huddlesford House and have a lovely view to your left of Lichfield's magnificent cathedral. Soon you will arrive at Bowman's Bridge over the Coventry canal. (To the north, the canal links with the Wyrley and Essington canal, that once provided a connection with the Black Country but it was abandoned in 1954 and became a mooring area for narrow boats.)

5 Cross the bridge and turn right to go over a stile down to the canal towpath. The towpath wanders through pleasant Staffordshire countryside, then passing a number of craft moored at the back of attractive homes, where there are some interesting gardens to look at. After about half a mile of easy walking you will arrive at bridge 80; here you leave the towpath to return to the Swan.

The Coventry canal

Date walk completed:

....

Place of Interest

Lichfield, 4 miles west, is the premier heritage site in Staffordshire and well worth a visit. The unique three-towered cathedral is surrounded by Bishop's Close. The city's main streets are set out in a medieval grid pattern, and the main street has many Georgian buildings. The city played a central role during the Civil War, suffering three sieges, and the cathedral sustained much damage. From the 18th century, Lichfield was the home of a number of well-known residents including Dr Samuel Johnson, Erasmus Darwin, David Garrick and Anna Seward. Telephone 01543 308209.

Alrewas

The Crown

In Old English Alrewas meant 'alluvial land where alders grow'. This small village, one of the most picturesque ancient villages in Staffordshire, is a winner of the Best Kept Village competition, and has a population of under 3,000. Many of its cottages are period buildings of traditional timber-frame construction, with attractive thatched roofs. The Trent and Mersey canal flows right through the heart of Alrewas. After an outward journey by the very beautiful canal, the return route takes you along the banks of the river Trent, which flows through the north and east side of the village. On your way back to the village you will be able to enjoy the picture-postcard scene of the unusual weir.

Distance: *3¼ miles*

OS Explorer 245
GR 171150

An easy walk along a towpath and river banks

Starting point: The Crown, Post Office Road, Alrewas

How to get there: Alrewas is situated off the A38 road, 6 miles north-east of Lichfield.

The **Crown** – this dream picture pub – is adorned with flowers during the summer months, and it is little wonder that it is a Midlands winner of the Pub in Bloom competition. Built in the 15th century, it is full of character. In the days when the mail coach called there, one snug room was used for distribution of the post. Like many other village inns, this one had its own malthouse and brewed its own ale. Today, the Crown is a popular eating place. There is a full menu of bar snacks and a specials board. Walkers may eat their own sandwiches in the garden if they purchase drinks in the pub.

Opening times *are from 11 am to 3 pm and from 5 pm to 11 pm, Monday to Saturday, and from 12 noon to 3 pm and from 7 pm to 10.30 pm on Sunday. Food is available from 12 noon to 2 pm and from 6 pm to 9.30 pm, Monday to Saturday, and from 12 noon to 2.30 pm and from 7 pm to 9 pm on Sunday.*

Telephone: *01283 790328.*

The Walk

❶ From the Crown car park, go left down Post Office Road to reach Main Street in Alrewas. Turn right, walk up to the bridge over the Trent and Mersey canal, and then go down onto the towpath, heading left (north-eastwards). You will soon pass beneath bridge no. 48 and then pass the narrowboats moored near lock no. 12. Now go over a series of footbridges. Shortly after you have passed lock 12, you will see the river Trent flowing in from the left, and, for about 220 yards, the river and the canal become one; a raised walkway that takes you past the weir. The river Trent continues east over the weir, but you continue along the towpath that bends left. Soon you will see Cow Bridge ahead of you.

❷ About 20 yards before reaching the bridge, leave the towpath and go left up a footpath in order to visit St Leonard's church and the tiny village of Wychnor. Return to the towpath, which you

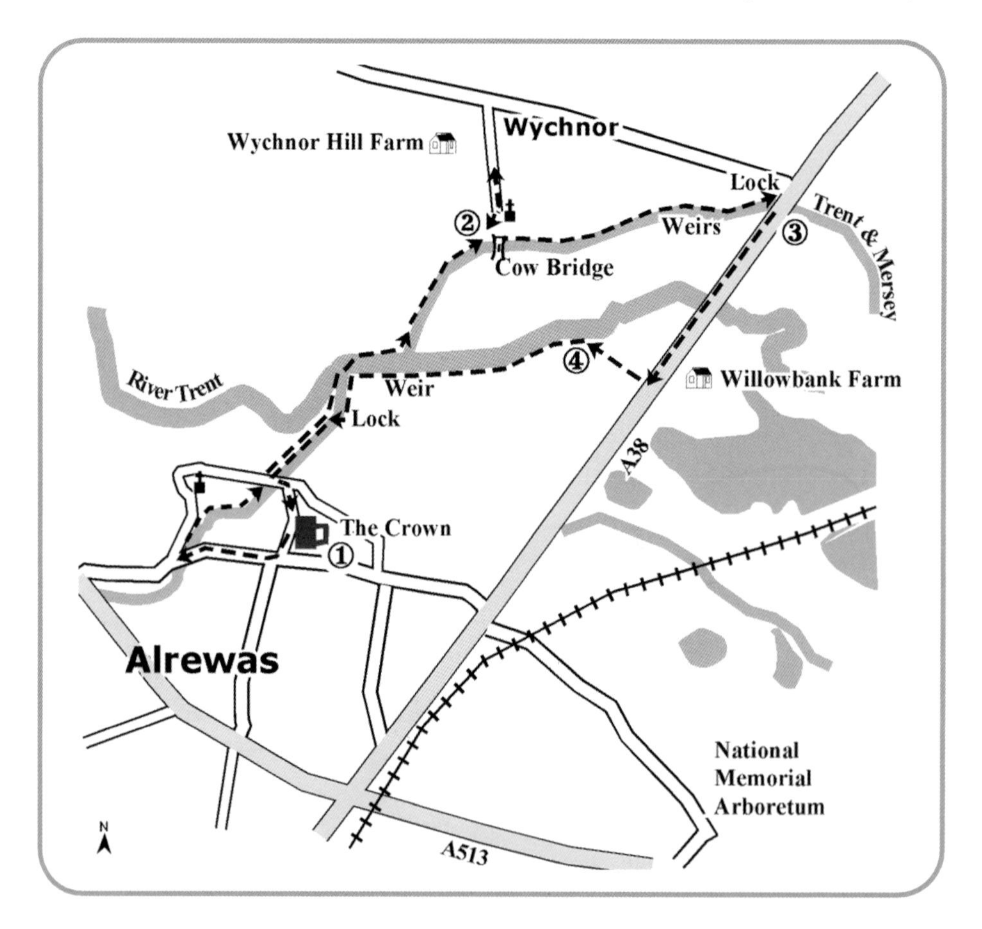

On the route

continue to follow. You will pass beneath Cow Bridge, where colourful narrowboats are moored. On August bank holiday each year there is a boat festival at Wychnor, and large numbers of colourful boats arrive to fill the canal. Go over the Wychnor bridge (no. 43) to arrive at the A38.

3 Turn right and walk along the pavement for about 600 yards. About 100 yards beyond the road bridge over the river Trent, turn right and go over the waymarked stile into a new woodland area. The footpath follows the hedge, but it is permitted to walk across the grass field to reach the banks of the river.

4 When you reach the river, turn left and stroll along the clear, well-used footpath along the river bank. The path hugs the river bank as you go over a stile. (Wychnor's St Leonard's church stands proud to the right. This is pleasant riverside walk, and you are likely to see a variety of wild birds: swans, seagulls, moorhens, coots, etc.) After passing the weir, you will reach lock 12 again and may be lucky enough to see a narrowboat negotiating the lock gates, always a colourful event. Cross over the lock gate; now walk along the towpath, back to bridge no. 48. Go up to Park Road in Alrewas and turn left to go over the canal bridge. Now turn right into Post Office Road to return to the Crown. You will pass a most attractive thatched cottage just before reaching the inn.

Place of Interest

The National Memorial Arboretum, 1 mile east, is a living tribute to the people of the 20th century. One can stroll around 150 acres of the nation's newest tree collection and admire a growing array of sculptures, perhaps visiting the Millennium Chapel of Peace and Forgiveness. Telephone: 01283 792333.

Date walk completed:

....

Walk 30 *Tatenhill*

The Horseshoe

Offering a variety of things to enjoy, this is a walk of great interest. You pass through new woodland and stroll on the banks of the Trent and Mersey canal and in Branston Water Park. The route continues along footpaths across farmland, passing Dunstall Hall, the attractive home of Sir Stanley Clarke, and entering the pretty village of Dunstall. More good views await as you climb above Tatenhill and then descend along good footpaths to arrive back at the Horseshoe.

Distance: *6 miles*

OS Explorer 245
GR 204219

An undulating walk on footpaths and tracks

Starting point: The car park of the Horseshoe in Tatenhill

How to get there: Tatenhill is 4½ miles west of Burton upon Trent. Leave Burton on the A5121, cross over the A38 and follow the signs to Tatenhill, driving along the Branston road. Turn right in the village to reach the Horseshoe.

The **Horseshoe** was built in 1680. It has great character and is a pleasure to visit, with a fine large garden to enjoy in summer. You will be guaranteed a warm welcome and excellent food, ranging from 'lite bites' to full meals, including a two-course OAP special.

***Opening times** are from 11 am to 11 pm (10.30 pm on Sunday) every day. Food is available between noon and 9.30 pm (9 pm on Sunday).*

***Telephone:** 01283 564913.*

The Walk

1 Leave the car park, and turn right through the village. About 250 yards after passing the church of St Michael and All Angels, turn right and follow the fingerpost direction on a footpath to the left of a cottage. Go over the stile and follow the direction of the sign 'Monks and Moorlands/Battlehead and Back' into the woodland of the Bass Millennium Wood, which is controlled by The Woodland Trust. Walk on a clear footpath through the attractive woodland, ignoring the sign to the left. Continue to a stile on the edge of the trees. (There is a clear view overlooking the Bass factory, a power station and the lakes at Branston.) Go down a wide track, crossing a metal stile to arrive at the corner of a road near Lawns Cottage. Turn left, and walk down the side of the road for about 20 yards; then cross over to pass through a kissing gate onto a permissive path set to the right of the roadside hedge. This path leads across two fields. Soon you will arrive at the Trent and Mersey canal; turn left and cross Branston Bridge

2 Turn right and descend to the towpath, heading past the Bridge Inn. In about 200 yards, Branston Water Park is to the left, and you can choose to walk along either the towpath or the path inside the Water Park; there are regular exits back onto the towpath. Continue southwards until you reach Tatenhill lock.

3 Turn right and cross the canal bridge. Then go along a pretty hedged footpath. Soon there will be a stretch of water on

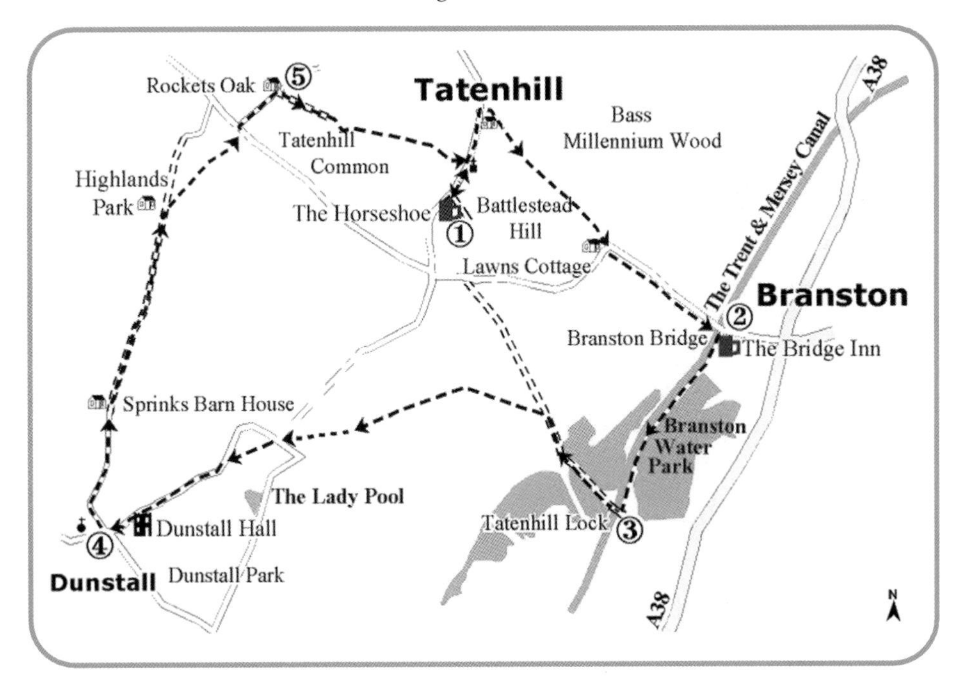

each side of the path, and then you will arrive in open countryside, walking on a wide grass track to the left of the hedge. When you reach the end of the second field, look out for a fingerpost and footpath going off to your left. Go over the stile and follow the fingerpost direction, crossing a cultivated field to a gap in the hedge. The next waymark directs you to a second hedge gap, by trees, as you continue, now in a south-westerly direction. Continue along the footpath (a fine view of Dunstall Hall emerges ahead of you), diagonally crossing a field to reach a road junction on the approach to Dunstall. Cross the road and go over the stile opposite, taking the footpath going right, to arrive back on the road. Turn left, and walk up the side of this quiet country road into the village of Dunstall. (You will have an exceptionally good view of the hall.) Continue past the entrance gate to the hall, and in a few yards you will reach a road junction.

4 Turn right up the tarmac lane towards Sprinks Barn Farm. (The village church is to the left.) In about 650 yards you pass to the right of Sprinks Barn House and go through the farm gate onto a clear grass track. This takes you past the end of a short avenue of trees and up a footpath through a cultivated field. When you reach the tarmac track that leads to the buildings of Highlands Park, pass to the right of them, following a waymarker to a stile. Then cross a cultivated field to reach what used to be the keeper's cottage on the estate. You will pass a couple of cottages and soon arrive at a road. Turn left, and then go right, down Cuckoo Gate Road.

Near Tatenhill

5 Opposite a cottage called Rockets Oak, turn right along a hedged farm track. This leads to a pair of kissing gates, and soon you will have a nice open view overlooking Tatenhill, Bass Millennium Wood and the industrial area surrounding Branston. Follow the footpath set to the right of the field hedge, going through several gates. Soon Tatenhill will be below you, and you should take the better path, that leads to a kissing gate to the left of the church. Turn right along the road to return to the Horseshoe.

Place of Interest

Coors Visitor Centre, Horninglow Street, Burton upon Trent, 4½ miles east. Formerly the Bass Museum, it is the UK's premier brewing museum, with shire horse stables, a museum of micro brewery, authentic cooperage, a vintage vehicle collection and a working stationary steam engine. Telephone: 01283 513613.

Date walk completed:

....

Penn

The Barley Mow

Enjoy this delightful easy walk along the edge of a golf course and along good footpaths in attractive countryside. It passes near to Baggeridge Country Park, and you may wish to extend your walk into this beautiful area of countryside on the doorstep of the Black Country. Baggeridge Park was once owned by the Earl of Dudley, who lived at nearby Himley Hall. In 1895 coal was discovered at the northern end of Baggeridge, pit shafts were sunk, and it became one of the world's biggest and most modern pits. The mine was nationalized in 1947, and eventually closed in 1968. Today it is an attractive leisure area for local people.

Built about 1630, the **Barley Mow** has low doorways and oak beams, and is situated in delightful countryside near to England's second city. As well as a warm welcome there are fresh and wholesome meals of large proportion; award-winning pies are among the favourites.

Opening times *are from 12 noon to 2.30 pm and 6 pm to 11 pm during the week, and from 12 noon to 11 pm (10.30 pm on Sunday) at the weekend. Food is served from 12 noon to 2 pm (3 pm on Sunday) and from 6 pm to 8.45 pm (no food on Sunday evening).*

Telephone: *01902 333510.*

Distance: *3 miles*

OS Explorer 219
GR 901950

A short easy off-road walk

Starting point: The Barley Mow pub on Pennmoor Common

How to get there: Approach Penn along the A449 Stourbridge road, turning right at the traffic island onto Penn Road. Take the third turn on the right (Vicarage Road), and continue past Penn church into Pennwood Lane. The Barley Mow is to the right, at the end of the lane.

The Walk

❶ From the car park at the Barley Mow, turn right. Go through the car park to the Penn Golf Club and follow the clear footpath on the left of the course (i.e. near to the hedge), walking down towards Penn Brook.

❷ Just after passing the fourth green, turn right and stroll along the bottom of the course until you reach a lane by a house. Go along the lane towards three further houses. Just before the first of them, Holly Cottage, turn left and go over the stile. Cross the footbridge over the brook and then go up, following the waymarker direction and going over further stiles. (On the horizon ahead, you will now see the tall chimney of Baggeridge Brickworks.) Walk on the pleasant footpath along the top of the

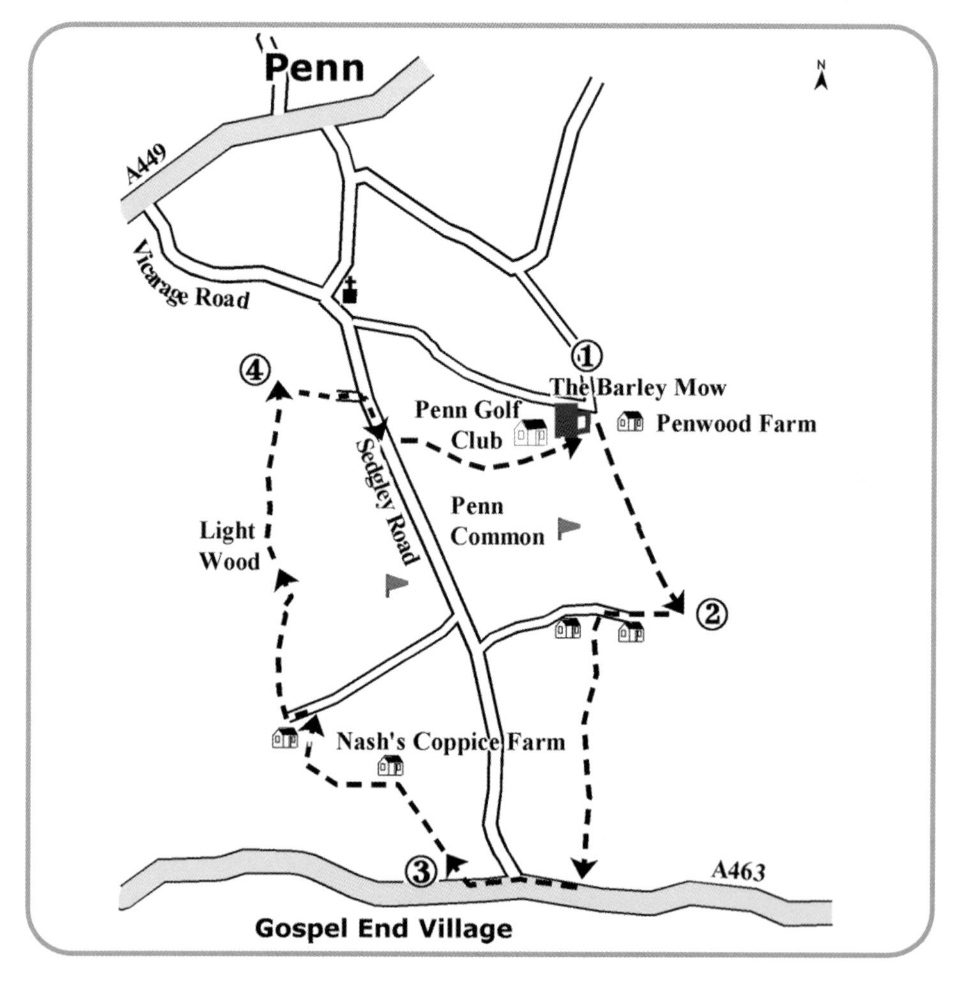

bank that is to the left of a row of hawthorn bushes. Very soon you will see the houses in Gospel End Village. Aim for the gap between the houses and go over the stile and up the hedged path to arrive on the main road in the village. Turn right and go along the pavement, past the junction with Penn Road.

❸ Opposite the entrance to Baggeridge Country Park, turn right and go over a stile into open countryside. Follow the waymarker directions into the valley, initially walking by the side of the field hedge. Eventually, the footpath arcs left, and you walk near to the building of Nash's Coppice Farm (behind the hedge to your right). The path bends right, and you go across a footbridge over a stream to arrive on the edge of a house where caravans are stored in a field. Walk on the path to the right of the buildings, passing through a paddock to a stile by a gate. Soon you will reach a lane, which you cross, bearing left to join the track that runs to the left of the first hole over the golf course. The track curves right into woodland, and you will reach a well-used track, which you follow to a junction of tracks. Here go left over a stile into a field and walk on the footpath to the right of the hedge, with Light Wood to the left. Continue over several stiles.

On the way to Gospel End

❹ Just after passing beneath the electricity cables, you will reach a hedge with a path junction beyond. Turn right just before the hedge and walk to the right of it over two more fields. Now bear left to pass to the left of the pylon and arrive in Cotsdale Road. At the T-junction, turn right and go down Sedgley Road. In about 200 yards, turn left along a lane past the last houses on the left; this will lead you back onto Penn Common. Continue to the right of the trees and pass to the right of the golf clubhouse, walking through the car park to arrive back at the Barley Mow.

Date walk completed:

....

Places of Interest

Broadfield House Glass Museum, Kingswinford, 4 miles south, displays world-famous collections of the very best British glass. Telephone: 01384 812745.

Black Country Living Museum, 3 miles south-east, is an open-air museum containing examples of vernacular historic buildings from all around the Black Country that have been reconstructed and preserved there. Telephone: 01215 579643.

Walk 32 Leasowes Park

The Black Horse, Illey

Leasowes Park comprises over 140 acres of parkland – a mixture of woodland, grassland, streams and lakes – designed by William Shenstone, who was born at the Leasowes in 1714. This lovely walk passes the golf course in Leasowes Park, and then makes its way through an attractive residential area. As the route progresses into the countryside, there are pleasing views to be enjoyed on the way to a welcoming inn. Attractive scenery leads past the ruins of an old abbey, and then the walk joins the towpath of an old feeder canal on the way back to Leasowes Park.

Distance: *4¼ miles*

OS Explorer 219
GR 975840

A pleasant walk along good footpaths

Starting point: The car park in Leasowes Park

How to get there: From Dudley, go down Mucklow Hill on the A458 towards Halesowen. Just after passing the traffic island near the B&Q store, turn left down the lane signed to Leasowes Park.

Built in 1872, the **Black Horse** at Illey offers the warmest of welcomes and the best of food, which you can choose from snack or à la carte menus. (The hot steak off the grill may appeal.)

Opening times *are from 11 am to 11 pm, Monday to Saturday, and from noon to 10.30 pm on Sunday. Food is available from 11 am to 10 pm every day (noon to 9.30 pm on Sunday).*

Telephone: *0121 550 2915.*

The Walk

1 From the car park, head along the tarmac driveway past the warden's building. At the lane junction turn right through a gateway, and continue along the driveway, passing a small pool and walking between the greens below the clubhouse of Halesowen Golf Club. The tarmac track arcs left towards the clubhouse, but you turn right into a residential area: Leasowes Lane. At the end of the lane, turn right along the pavement of Manor Lane (the B4043). After passing Stennels Avenue, the lane bends sharp right, and here you go left up a narrow 'fenced' footpath to the right of house no. 61 to arrive in Hiplands Road. Turn right, go right again into Manor Abbey Road, and then, in about 20 yards, turn left down Longlands Road. Pass Lavina and Christopher roads, and then go left through a pubic footpath barrier to reach the A456 Halesowen bypass, which you cross at the pedestrian crossing. Walk along the verge of Lapal Lane opposite for about 300 yards.

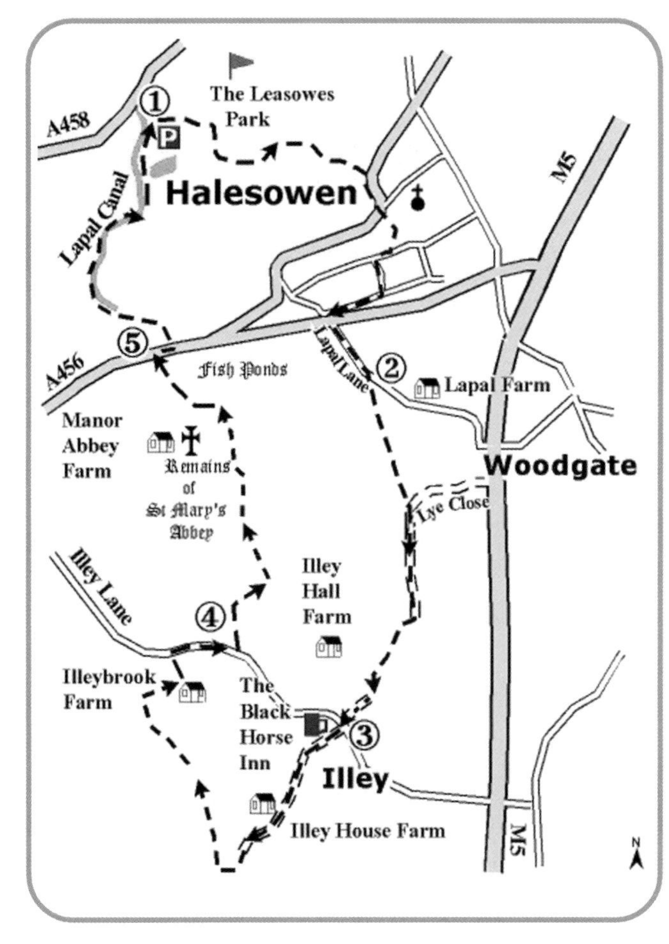

2 At the road bend, turn right and go over a field stile into open countryside. Follow the fingerpost in the direction of Illey, and climb the clear footpath along the left edge of the large cultivated field. (At the top, pause to enjoy the excellent view embracing the Wychbury, Clent and Clee Hills to the right.) Turn left over a second stile and then bend right onto a hedged path, which becomes a track where Lye Close comes in from the left. Continue ahead at the junction of paths and pass to the left of Cooper's Wood. At the end of the wood, turn right through a farm gate and then bear right, crossing pastureland through a gap in the hedge. The path arcs right and left, and then becomes a farm track, which you continue along to the Black Horse.

Breaches Pool

3 At the end of the inn car park, turn right and head up the footpath/ lane (signed to Romsley and Waseley) for about half a mile, passing Illey House Farm and crossing over a stream before ascending through a farm gate into open countryside. After crossing another stream, climb the bank, and turn right, following the Illey Way/Monarch's Way signs. The path tends to follow the line of the stream. After crossing another footpath, climb over a series of stiles as Illeybrook Farm appears to the right. At a junction of paths, turn right and climb up to a stile set to the left of the farm. Head left down the farm drive to Illey Lane; then turn right, and, with care, walk at its side for about 300 yards.

4 Cross the lane and go left over a stile onto the Monarch's Way. The footpath hugs the hedge, and in about 150 yards (mid-field) you follow the waymarker, heading right towards a stile in the hedge. Go over the stile, bearing left. (There is a stream to the right.) The path then bends right to a footbridge and becomes a farm track leading towards Manor Abbey Farm. Bear right, away from the farm, going over a corner stile and continuing over a large cultivated field towards an area of fishponds (in former quarry pits). Turn left over the stile, go right over a footbridge, and walk to the A456 road. (The remains of St Mary's Abbey are visible behind you.)

5 Head right along the side of the busy A456 road for about 25 yards; then cross at the pedestrian crossing. Turn right, and then left along a tarmac footpath signed 'Leasowes Park and Breaches Pool'. You will walk along the back of residential properties and soon join the Lapal canal towpath. (The canal is covered with water plants and there are houses up to the right.) After about 400 yards, cross over a bank of grass and continue along the towpath, walking to the right of the canal, with Leasowes Park to the right. In 150 yards, pause to enjoy the fine view over Breaches Pool, and then continue to the Leasowes car park and visitor centre.

Place of Interest

Dudley Zoological Gardens, 6 miles north, offer a fine collection of animals set against the feudal splendour of castle ruins. Telephone: 01384 215313.

Date walk completed:

....

The Dudley Port

An easy walk along the towpath of the Birmingham canal provides an opportunity to experience a little of the industrial past of the area. Until the 18th century, Birmingham was a small and relatively insignificant settlement on the banks of the river Rea. With the arrival of the Industrial Revolution, the city expanded rapidly as it exploited its position at the crossroads of developing canal and river systems which extended from London to Liverpool and from Bristol to the Humber estuary. In Victorian times, the canal system was the motorway of its day, and it is fascinating to explore the clever two-tier plan. Essentially, the Birmingham canal is built on two levels, with a second, main canal (engineered by Thomas Telford) cut 20 ft lower than an earlier winding channel.

Distance: *5¼ miles*

OS Explorer 219
GR 964913

An easy, level walk

Starting point: The car park of the Dudley Port

How to get there: Dudley is 7¾ miles north-west of the centre of Birmingham. Follow the A457 road across the city towards Dudley. The pub is set off the A461 road.

The **Dudley Port** is a typical Mr Q pub, set in a Victorian building with a smart modern interior. The pub serves an extensive range of the best beers around and good pub food. You can choose from one of two menus throughout the day. Although not a country pub, there is a good atmosphere and locals and visitors are given a warm welcome.

Opening times *when both food and drink are available, are from 11 am to 11 pm, Monday to Saturday, and noon to 10.30 pm on Sunday.*

Telephone: *0121 5571410.*

The Walk

1 From the car park, go down Dudley Port Road to the viaduct carrying the main line of the Birmingham canal. Climb the steps up onto the towpath of the canal, turn right, and then continue along the towpath, going generally south-east. (This is easy walking; so take time to absorb the general scene.) After about 450 yards, cross a footbridge by the Stoke End Works canal bridge at Dudley Port Junction. (If you look right along the stretch of the Netherton Tunnel branch, you can see the canal disappearing into the hills.) Continue for a further mile to arrive at the Gower branch.

2 Turn right and walk down the left side of the Gower Branch along its towpath. You will pass a lock gate and go beneath the A457. By the side of lock gates, climb up to reach a more winding part of the canal.

3 Turn right and go over a footbridge to continue, now walking generally north-westwards. You will pass beneath a series of road bridges and will see some industrial buildings to the left as you progress. After about half a mile, cross over Tividale Aqueduct, at the other end of the Netherton Tunnel branch, to get a clear view of the tunnel disappearing into the bank on its way to Windmill End Junction, where it links with the Staffordshire and Worcestershire canal. Continue along the towpath and enjoy the

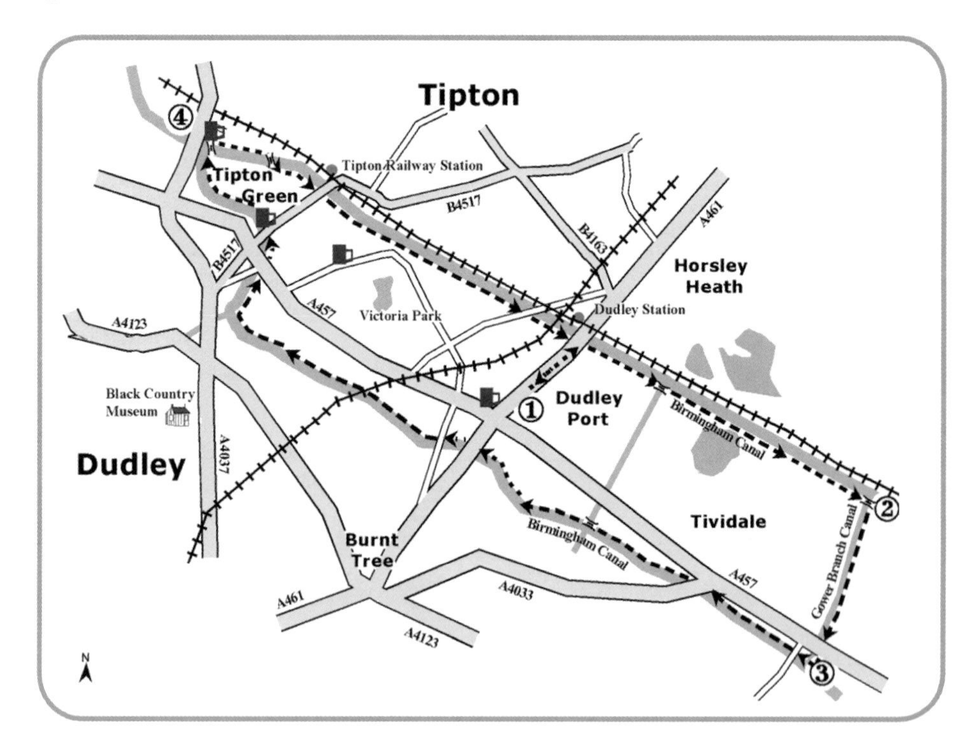

Stoke End Works canal bridge

pleasant scene, passing by some residential properties. Shortly after going beneath Pitchfork Bridge, the canal bends right as you continue along the towpath. To the left is a spur off to the Black Country Living Museum, and you may see some of the old steam narrowboats manoeuvring to enter their docking place. As you continue, you pass beneath Tipton Green and Owen Green bridges. The canal curves left, and soon you cross a footbridge near to the Barge and Barrel pub in Factory Road. (There is a nice garden by the canal, if you are ready for a pint.)

❹ Turn right and continue along the left-bank towpath past Factory Lock gates. Then cross over onto the right bank. After passing Tipton railway station, the route goes beneath the B4517 road bridge. You will pass more factories and beneath a pipe bridge to arrive back at Dudley Port roadbridge. (Dudley Port railway station is to the left.) Go down to the road and make your way to the Dudley Port pub.

Place of Interest

Black Country Living Museum is an open-air museum containing examples of vernacular historic buildings from all around the Black Country that have been reconstructed and preserved there. Telephone: 01215 579643.

Date walk completed:

....

Walk 34 Walsall Wood

The Boatman's Rest

This is a delightful easy excursion along part of the towpath of the the Wyrley and Essington canal, that runs for almost 17 miles from Wolverhampton to Brownhills, skirting the northern Birmingham canal navigations. It is aptly nicknamed the Curley Wyrley, because of its twisting course. After a short stretch along the towpath, the route takes you into attractive countryside and past the site of former Pelsall Iron Works, now converted into a superb leisure area. After crossing Clayhanger Common, you return to the towpath to complete your walk.

Distance: *5½ miles*

OS Explorer 244
GR 045030

An easy walk

Starting point: The car park of the Boatman's Rest, High Street, Walsall Wood

How to get there: From the A5 road drive along the A461 into Walsall Wood. After passing the church on your right, you will soon reach the Boatman's Rest on the right, just before the canal bridge.

Built in the early 1900s, the **Boatman's Rest** was once a traditional canal-side pub, which today has retained much of that flavour while adapting to the modern world. Good food and a good selection of beers are the order of the day. The real ales are Banks' Original and Bitter, plus various guest ales. The excellent food is provided in the pub by John's Galley, from a reasonably priced menu or the specials board.

Opening times *are from noon to 11 pm (10.30 pm on Sunday). Food is available from noon to 2 pm (3 pm on Sunday) and from 5.30 pm to 8.30 pm (6 pm to 9 pm on Sunday).*

Telephone: *01543 454995.*

The Walk

1 From the Boatman's Rest pub, go onto High Street in Walsall Wood, and turn right. Walk over the canal road bridge and then cross over the busy A461 with care. Go down the stairway to reach the towpath of the Wyrley and Essington canal. Then turn left and walk beneath the road bridge and along the pleasant towpath until you reach Blackcock Bridge.

2 Walk beneath the bridge and turn sharp left to leave the towpath onto Green Lane. Head right along the pavement, passing the Black Cock pub. After walking along the lane for about 500 yards, you will reach a bend by a small copse. Turn right and enter the copse through the kissing gate. Continue through the trees on a clear wide grass path. Leave the copse over a stile and continue over pastureland to arrive at a pair of stiles that take you over the driveway to Grange Farm. Follow the waymarker direction over a couple of fields, keeping to the right-hand edge. You will pass through gaps in the hedge and will eventually arrive at a hand gate in the

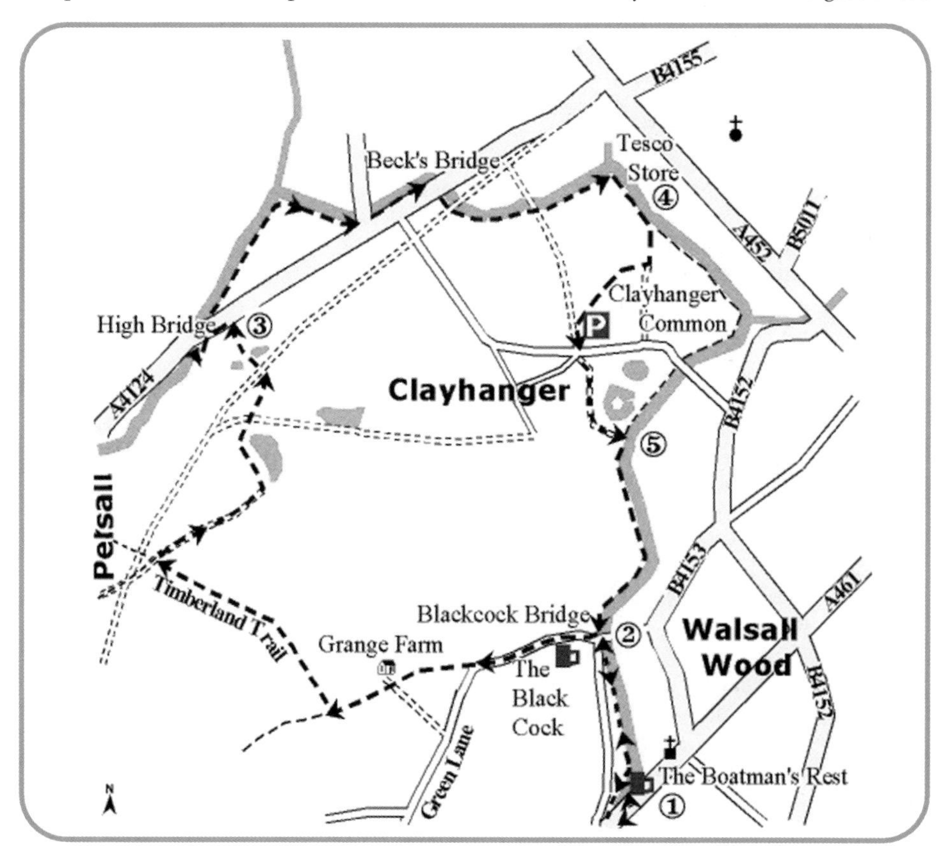

corner of the field. Go through the gate and turn left along a farm track.

At the end of this field, the track arcs right. You walk on the other side of the hedge, with the village of Pelsall now visible ahead to your left. A stile leads onto a good gravel footpath (the Timberland Trail), and you walk to the right of the field hedge for the next 500 yards. After passing a farm gate you reach a junction of footpaths; turn right. (Once there was a farm to the right, but this has gone, as have Pelsall Iron Works.) Soon you will reach a large man-made lake. The footpath arcs left, close to the lake, where swans, ducks, and Canada geese enjoy the large expanse of water. Go over a stile, crossing a dismantled railway track that leads to some of the former workings (now lakes). Then pass beneath a former railway bridge to enjoy some smaller pools, where bulrushes line the banks. Go ahead – do not take the path that arcs right – and within a few yards you will reach a stile onto the A4124 road.

❸ Turn left along the pavement; then bear left just before High Bridge (a canal bridge), where you drop down to the towpath. Turn right beneath the bridge for another stretch (about 1½ miles) of pleasant walking by the canal, passing beneath several road bridges and by a Tesco store on the far bank. (There are rippling reflections to enjoy, and you are likely to pass a number of fishermen in pursuit of the pike, carp, tench, roach, perch and bream that frequent these waters. I saw three small pike when I completed the walk.)

❹ About 250 yards beyond the Tesco store, pass beneath a footbridge, and then turn right to leave the towpath. Follow a tarmac footpath towards Clayhanger Common. In about 250 yards, the path bends left; here you bear right, and continue along an earth pathway which will lead you past the car park to arrive at the main entrance to the common. Leave the common and cross the road. Go through a kissing gate and follow the clear footpath that initially bends right. (Below, to the left, you will see another attractive lake where birds are at play.) The path arcs left and soon you will arrive back at the towpath.

Swans on the Wyrley and Essington canal

❺ Turn right and continue along the towpath. After passing under Blackcock Bridge, retrace your steps along the towpath to the Boatman's Rest, where refreshments await.

Place of Interest

Walsall Arboretum, 4 miles south-west, is a beautiful Victorian park, famous for its illuminations. Telephone: 01922 653141.

Date walk completed:

....

Cannon Hill Park 35 Walk

The Selly Park Tavern

A stroll around beautiful Cannon Hill Park is a delightful way to spend an afternoon. This is Birmingham's most beautiful park and you will enjoy seeing its many flowerbeds, lakes and pools, and wonderful trees. The tropical greenhouses at Cannon Hill are home to the national collection of *Codiaeum.* The conservation area includes five acres of woodland known as the RSPB Centenary Plantation, and there is a wildflower meadow, which is sown each year with cornfield annuals such as field poppy, cornflower and corn marigold. Birds and squirrels are common in the park, and you are likely to see mistle thrushes, jackdaws, goldfinches, willow warblers, pied wagtails and tufted ducks.

Distance: *3½ miles*

OS Explorer 220
GR 066840

An easy walk

Starting point: The car park opposite Edgbaston cricket ground

How to get there: Cannon Hill Park is 2½ miles south of the centre of Birmingham. Take the A440 from the city and continue along the A441; then follow the Cannon Hill Park signs. Entrance is opposite the Edgbaston cricket ground.

The **Selly Park Tavern**, an impressive tall building, was once a 19th-century coaching inn but was rebuilt in 1901 and has earned a reputation for good food and ales (such as the Ember brand of M&B real ale). Food is available every day, and you can select from menus of sandwiches, salads, bar snacks or à la carte. The steak and Ember ale pie is particularly popular, and the Sunday roasts are special – but you will enjoy the food whatever your choice. It is very pleasant to sit outside on the patio.

Opening times *are from 12 noon to 11.30 pm (10.30 pm on Sunday). Food is available from 12 noon to 8 pm each day.*

Telephone: *0121 414 9941.*

The Walk

1 From the car park, cross the footbridge over the river Rea into Cannon Hill Park; then turn left and head along the side of the first of several lakes in the park. Take your time to enjoy the attractive scene, where many ducks, geese, moorhens and coots add to the pleasing picture; you may be lucky enough to see a heron. Walk to the superb working scale model of the Elan Valley reservoirs.

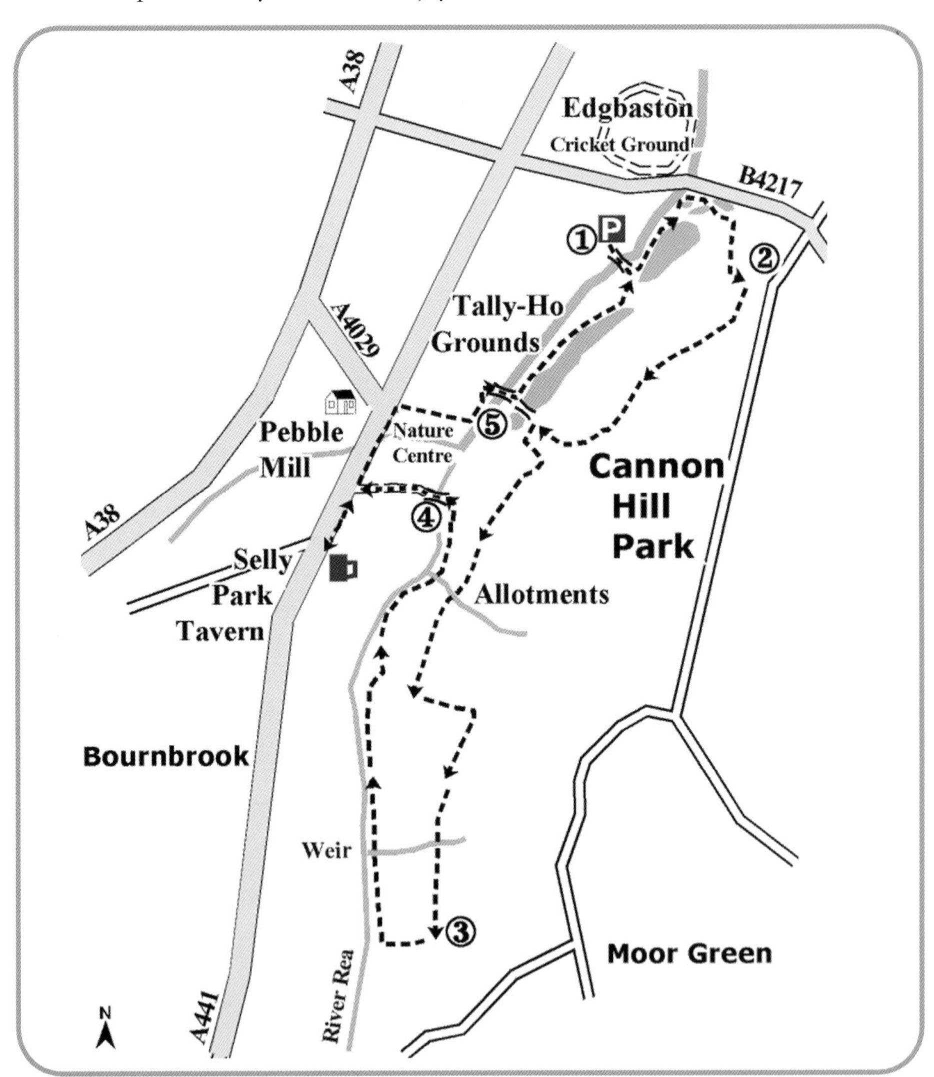

The model was built in 1961 to remind Birmingham of the beautiful Elan reservoirs, which were built over 100 years ago to provide water for the city. On an average day some 365 million litres of water travel the 73 miles by gravity to the city.

Continue, bearing gently right, past the war memorial to soldiers lost in South Africa at the end of the 19th century. As you progress you will reach the tearooms and the information centre, and may wish to relax with a cuppa.

2 Continue along the tarmac path through the park, passing the band stand and the superb old building that was once the Golden Lion pub, a beautiful half-timbered Elizabethan building which was dismantled and moved here from Deritend (Digbeth) in 1911. The path curves left, and soon you reach a bridge over the river Rea. Here, bear left and proceed onto the well-used footpath that goes along the back of the toilet block. The path takes you along the side of allotment gardens and through a mix of trees and shrubs until you arrive back on the tarmac pathway. Now head left, up into the woodland area of the park. In about 100 yards, bear right and go along the park footpath through lovely deciduous trees, which are quite a picture in the autumn.

3 At the end of the woodland, go right to reach a footpath; head right again up the path, walking by the side of the river. After about 650 yards of pleasant, easy walking, you will arrive at a bridge over the river.

4 Here, go left and walk up an access road to the A441. The Selly Park Tavern

Cannon Hill Park

is up the road to your left. When you have refreshed yourself, retrace your steps past the access road near to the former BBC broadcasting centre in Pebble Mill. After passing the nature centre, turn right through the car park to reach the lane at its rear that runs by the side of the river. Head left along this lane for about 100 yards; then go right and cross a bridge over the river to re-enter Cannon Hill Park.

5 Do not go over the footbridge in the park, but head left along the side of the largest of the park's lovely lakes. This will lead you past the main buildings and back to the entrance bridge, where you to leave the park on your way back to the car park.

Place of Interest
Cadbury World, Bournville, 4 miles south-west, comprises the Cadbury Brothers' factory and the Bournville Garden village (www.cadbury.co.uk).

Date walk completed:

....

Walk 36 Sutton Park

Toby Carvery

Sutton Park, designated a National Nature Reserve in 1997 by English Nature, comprises 2,400 acres of wild countryside including marshes, seven lakes and extensive woodland. It is Birmingham's largest park and the glory of Sutton Coldfield. During the foot and mouth epidemic in 2001, the park was a lifesaver to walkers and we came from afar in large numbers to be able to continue walking in the countryside. The park has a long and fascinating history. Ancient Icknield Street runs across its corner, and the Normans hunted here. Shakespeare had kinsmen at Sutton and no doubt visited the superb park. Sir John Falstaff may well have brought his ragged army here, for he declared to Bardolph: 'Get thee before to Coventry; fill me a bottle of sack; our soldiers shall march through. We'll to Sutton Coldfield tonight.'

Distance: *7 miles*

OS Explorer 220
GR 112960

An easy, level walk

Starting point: The car park near to the visitor centre in Sutton Park

How to get there: Sutton Park is about 10 miles north of the centre of Birmingham, along the A38 and A5127 roads. In Sutton Coldfield, turn left into Park Road and pass beneath the railway bridge to reach the park.

A visit to any Toby inn is sure to satisfy, and when you visit the **Toby Carvery** in Sutton Park you will be impressed by the superb black and white building and surroundings, an idyllic place to rest and refresh. The food is excellent, my favourite being the honey and mustard glazed gammon, and there is a full menu from which to select, including a two-course carvery, which is very reasonably priced. The pub is well used by ramblers and local people in the area.

Opening times *are from 12 noon to 11 pm (10.30 pm on Sunday). Food is served at any time up until 10 pm (9 pm on Sunday).*

Telephone: *0121 354 2458.*

The Walk

1 Walk from the car park towards the entrance. Turn left and head up the road towards Keeper's Pool. At the end of the pool, bear right through a hand gate and walk along the edge of the pool; then bear left (northwards) through the trees, and walk on the clear path to reach Blackroot Pool. Walk along the left edge of this pool for 220 yards; then bear left (in a north-westerly direction), and continue along a clear track through the woodland of Upper Nut Hurst. After about half a mile of pleasant walking, turn right and cross the railway track to arrive at Bracebridge Pool, bearing right. Stroll along the edge of Bracebridge Pool, taking time to enjoy the lovely scene.

2 At the end of the pool, bear left and walk on the clear footpath through the trees. You will go over a series of footbridges. After about 300 yards, head right, away from the pool, following a fern-lined path through the trees. In a further 300 yards, the path arcs generally left, and you soon reach a junction of paths, where you turn left. Continue south-westwards, eventually going down to cross a footbridge at the northern end of Bracewell Pool. Follow the track as it

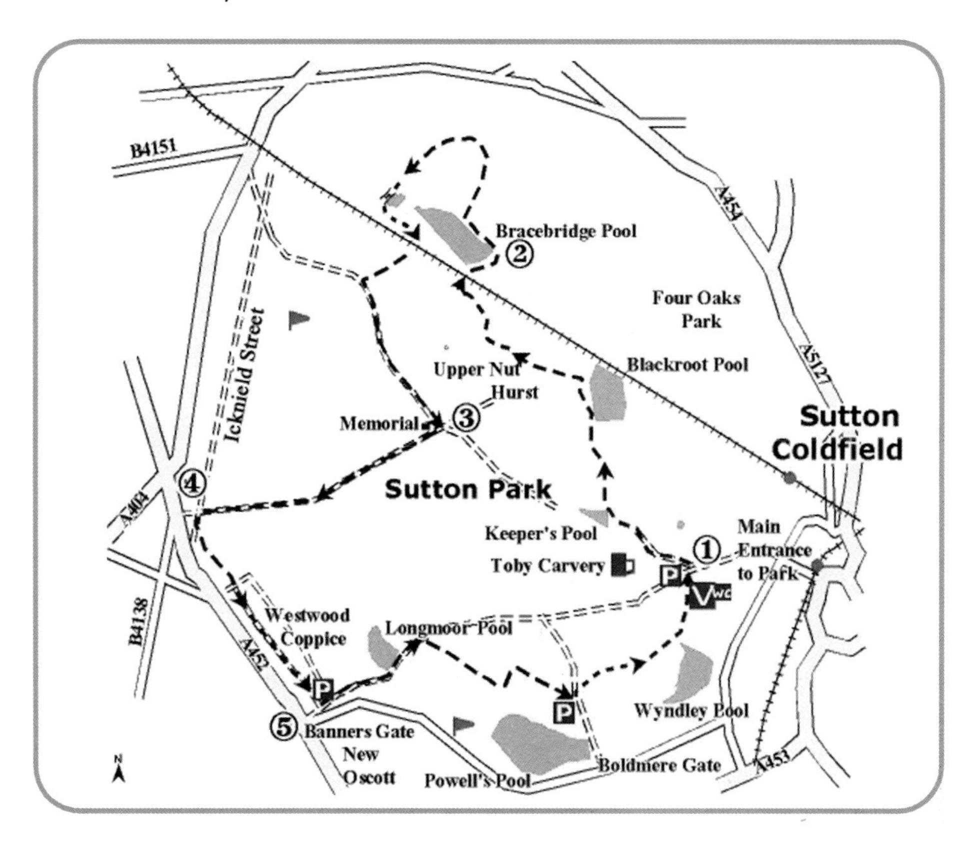

The Jamboree Memorial Stone in Sutton Park

bends left and then right. Soon you cross over the railway line again, to continue in a south-westerly direction along a good track and reach a park road. Turn left, and walk up the quiet road into the centre of Sutton Park.

3 Just after passing a memorial stone, turn right, and continue for about a mile along the road (now walking in a south-westerly direction), towards a park gateway.

4 About 100 yards before reaching the gateway, turn left onto a track, and then bear left again into the trees of Westwood Coppice. Walk through the trees, going in a south-easterly direction. After about half a mile, you will arrive at the car park by Banners Gate.

5 Here, turn left and go up the road past the car park. Continue to the right of Longmoor Pool. About 90 yards beyond the end of the pool, leave the road to bear right along the track and resume a south-easterly direction. Pass to the left of trees; then cross an open grass area to the north of Powell's Pool, to reach the roadway near Boldmere Gate. Head left along the road for 130 yards, and then bear right, through the edge of Wyndley Wood. In about 220 yards, bear right again; go along the straight road that leads to a cattle grid and ford situated at the end of Wyndley Pool. Continue ahead (north-east) to return to the car park near the visitor centre.

Place of Interest

Walsall Arboretum, 4 miles south-west, is a beautiful Victorian park, famous for its illuminations. Telephone: 01922 653141.

Date walk completed:

....

Solihull 37 Walk

The Masons' Arms

From Brueton Park, this easy walk takes you through residential estates into pastureland and down to the famous Grand Union canal. After walking along its fine towpath for about a mile, the route crosses over Copt Heath golf course, and then returns through a residential area to the park. If you have time, go into Solihull and stroll along High Street with its old timber-framed houses and shops; Tudor England appears to lurk around every corner. In St Alphege's church you can see a rare altar stone in the crypt and a brass portrait of William Hill (1549), who has with him two wives and their eighteen children.

Distance: *7 miles*

OS Explorer 220
GR 163788

A level easy walk

Starting point: Brueton Park car park

How to get there: Solihull is 8 miles south-east of Birmingham.

The Masons' Arms, situated on the edge of Solihull, specializes in 'classic pub food' and offers all day breakfast, steaks, salads, chips, bangers and mash, and several vegetarian choices. If you prefer a light snack, you could try a hot baguette filled with delicious steak and onions. There is a delightful garden for the warmer days.

Opening times *are 11 am to 11 pm, from Monday to Saturday, and from 12 noon to 10.30 pm on Sundays. Food is available between 11 am and 6 pm; and from 12 noon to 5 pm on Sunday.*

Telephone: *0121 7118041.*

The Walk

❶ Leave the car park in Brueton Park and walk along the drive to the road. Cross the road at the junction into Marsh Lane. Walk along the pavement of Marsh Lane until you reach a traffic island; go right, and then left into Avenbury Drive. Just before reaching the first house on the right, turn right through a kissing gate into open countryside, walking along the footpath to the right of the hedge over several fields. Now bear right over the stile into woodland, with Old Berry Hall hidden in the trees. Leave the woodland through a kissing gate and go ahead over Ravenshaw Lane; then continue to the right of the hedge. Go over several fields and stiles, and then bear left onto a stone track that takes you to the Grand Union Canal.

❷ Go down to the canal and turn right, heading southwards along the towpath. You will go beneath the M42 motorway and Barston Lane before leaving the canal at the next bridge.

❸ Cross the bridge and go over a stile onto a footpath going towards Grove Farm. Just after passing the farm, go left over a stile and follow a waymarked

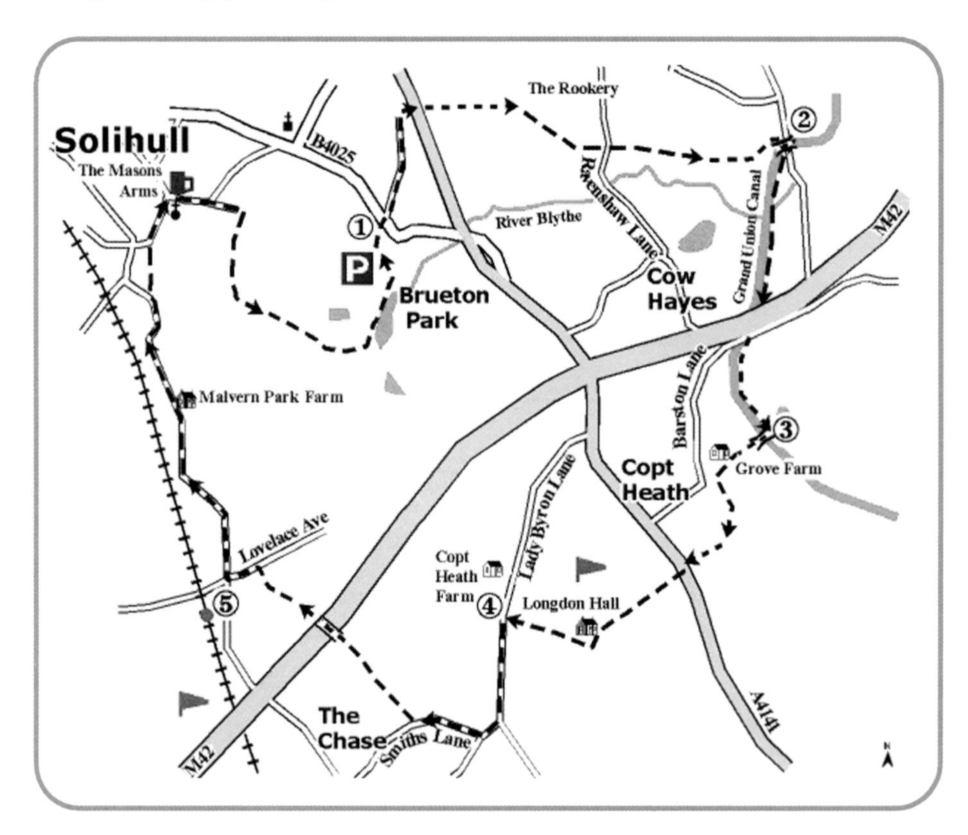

footpath and lanes, passing some attractive houses on the outskirts of Knowle. Cross over the A4141 Warwick road and continue on the public footpath. Cross Copt Heath golf course and soon arrive near to Longdon Hall. Immediately after passing the main entrance to the hall, go right and walk on a hedged footpath to arrive back on the golf course. Continue in a north-westerly direction, taking care not to interfere with the golf, to reach a stile into Lady Byron Lane.

Brueton Park Lake

4 Turn left here, and walk on the verge for about quarter of a mile, passing the many imposing houses. Turn right into Browns Lane, and, in about 100 yards, go right along the verge of Smiths Lane. After walking along the lane for about 325 yards, go right again over a stile into farmland and continue in a north-westerly direction, keeping to the left edge of the field until you go across a footbridge over the M42. Continue along the footpath, and go over a stile onto Lovelace Avenue.

5 Now go left, and then go right, up Widney Manor Road. At the road junction, turn right onto the pavement of Hillfield Road, soon to arrive on Church Hill Road, which bends left towards a traffic island. Turn right and continue up Church Hill Road, avoiding the busy traffic. Near the top is St Alphege's church, with the Masons' Arms opposite. Turn right into New Road and descend into Park Road. Turn right into Malvern Park through the main gate, and then bear immediately right and walk to the left of tennis courts. (There are some lovely flowerbeds here.) After passing the Prancing Horse and Man, bear left towards the main part of Malvern Park and walk on a tarmac footpath that gently curves left around the lovely trees. Past a teashop, you will soon reach a toilet block; walk to the right of it, to Brueton Park lake. Turn left, and walk on the tarmac path by the lake to arrive back in the car parking area.

Place of Interest

Packwood House (National Trust), 7 miles south-east, is a superb house, Tudor in origin but much restored in the 20th century. It is famous for its garden and topiary. Telephone: 01564 787924.

Date walk completed:

....

Walk 38 Marston Green

The Little Owl

This is an easy walk into attractive countryside surrounding an urban area. The walk takes you along lanes and on footpaths and tracks to and around Birmingham International Airport, and you will see how well many of the industrial estates are hidden from view.

Distance: *4½ miles*

OS Explorer 220
GR 179854

An easy town walk

Starting point: The recreation ground, Marston Green.

How to get there: Approach Marston Green from junction 6 of the M42. Drive along the A45 and turn right onto the B4438, following the signs for Marston Green. At the traffic island, turn left into Bickenhill Road; in about half a mile, you will find the recreation ground on the right.

The **Little Owl** has only been open for a short time, but has already attracted plenty of local custom, including some national personalities. It is only a short drive away, and you are assured of a good meal. The pub offers reasonably priced British food served in a traditional way, and the Sunday roast is something special.

Opening times *are from 11 am to 11 pm, Monday to Saturday; and from 12 noon to 10.30 pm on Sunday. Food is available from 12 noon to 10 pm (9.30 pm on Sunday).*

Telephone: *0121 781 0330.*

The Walk

1 From the car park at the recreation ground, walk back to the entrance in Bickenhall Road. Now turn left and walk along the pavement to a bend in the road, just after Eastwoodhay Guest House. Continue ahead along the tarmac entrance to the cemetery. At the corner, turn left, and then bear right to walk along the attractive footpath inside the Millennium Wood. As you bend right, the path runs almost parallel with the lane to the cemetery, and you will emerge in a small car park opposite the cemetery. Turn left and continue past the cemetery to reach a stile, which you cross. Turn right, walking on a clear wide grass path, initially along the side of the cemetery. At its end, continue straight ahead, passing along the boundary of domestic gardens to reach a stream. Now the path goes left and continues with Birmingham Park (it used to be called Elmdon Trading Estate) to the left and the railway line up to the right. (At first, the buildings are well hidden.) Then you walk along a fenced path. After about 350 yards, when level with the second large trading estate building, you will reach a stone bridge over the railway line, which you cross. (You will have a good view of Birmingham airport from here.)

2 At the other side of the bridge, turn right along a clear fenced track by the side of the airport. (You will have a good view of aircraft parked ready for taking

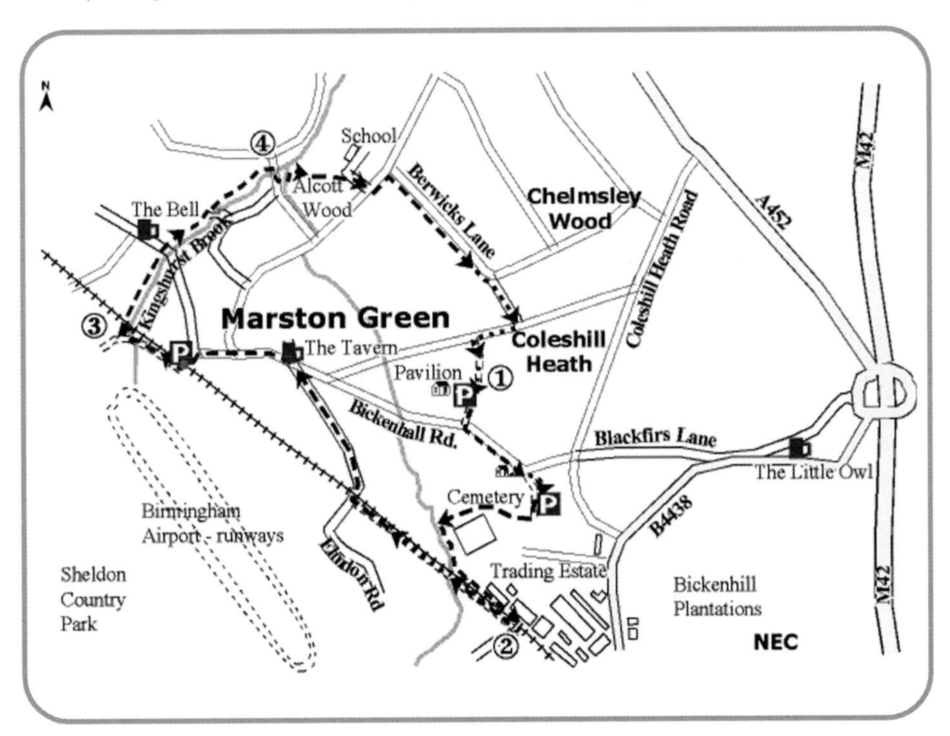

travellers all over the world, and will see the tall banking designed to protect residents nearby from the noise of aircraft landing and taking off.) Continue along this track, going over a footbridge and along the back of private houses. Soon you reach a railway bridge. Climb up to Elmdon Road; turn right, and cross the bridge. Then walk along the pavement in Elmdon Road until you reach the Centenary Clock, which was erected in 1994 to commemorate 100 years of local democracy. Turn left into Station Road and go through the centre of Marston Green, passing the Tavern Inn as the road bends left to the mainline railway station. Cross the footbridge over the line and go to the right along a tarmac footpath. (You may see aircraft taking off or landing on the runway to your left.) Go into Sheldon Country Park and descend to Hatchford Brook, which you cross over the footbridge; then bear right through bushes.

The Centenary Clock in Elmdon Road

3 At the crossing of several footpaths, turn right and pass beneath a railway arch. (This is the Solihull Way, although you may not find any waymarkers.) With the brook to your right, walk along this pleasant footpath for about half a mile, crossing over a busy road, where you will see the Bell Inn to your left. You can then walk along a tarmac lane (but I found it pleasant to walk along the grass bank to the right, nearer to the brook) until you come to the next bridge and Chapelhouse Road.

4 Turn right and cross over the bridge. Then turn left to reach an entrance to Alcott Wood. Turn right, enter the woodland, and walk on the clear path that bends left inside the wood. Soon you will be walking along the left edge of the largely deciduous wood and will emerge in Chichester Grove. Here, bear right and walk up to Moorhead Avenue. Cross Moorhead Avenue and go left along the wide grass verge; turn right into Berwicks Lane. Where the lane bends left, continue ahead, by the side of fencing, until you reach the Coleshill road. Here, turn right and walk on the pavement for about 200 yards. Opposite the entrance to Chelmsley Wood football pitch, turn left along the waymarked footpath that will lead you back to the recreation ground.

Place of Interest

Shustoke Reservoir, 6 miles north-east, is owned by Severn Trent Water and is the home of Shustoke Sailing Club. It is a lovely lake, which attracts many unusual visiting birds, including red necked grebe, osprey, hobby and buzzard. Telephone: 0182 2771 5341.

Date walk completed:

....

Berkswell

The Bear Inn

There can be few nicer places to visit than beautiful Berkswell, and this walk along part of the Heart of England Way into the surrounding area is a treat indeed. In autumn, the colourful leaves on the trees that line the walk offer a photo opportunity not to be missed. The superb 12th-century church of St John the Baptist is rather special, for it has a wonderful two-storey gabled and timbered porch dating from the 16th century. Although the nearby stocks were probably built with six holes, it is more amusing to believe the local legend that they were specially made to accommodate a one legged man and two drunken companions.

Distance: 5 miles

OS Explorer 221
GR 244791

An easy walk on good footpaths, tracks and lanes

Starting point: The car park by the church in the centre of Berkswell.

How to get there: Berkswell is 15 miles south-east of Birmingham, but is best approached on major roads. Take the A38 to the M6. Leave the M6 at junction 4 and go onto the A452. After 17½ miles, turn left and follow the signs to Berkswell.

Often described as 'the perfect example of the old English inn', the **Bear Inn** is a fine half-timbered pub that was once part of the Berkswell estate, and in 1874 was called the Bear and Ragged Staff. The Bear Inn is a regular haunt of local rambling groups and offers a warm welcome and good food.

Opening times *are from 11 am to 11 pm, Monday to Saturday, and 12 noon to 10.30 pm on Sunday. Food is available up until 10 pm (9.30 pm on Sunday).*

Telephone: *01676 533202.*

The Walk

1 Leave the village car park through a hand gate at its rear and bear right through the trees to reach the Meriden road. Cross the road and head up the pavement for about 300 yards; then turn right and walk along a hedged track called Blind Hall Lane. This clear, easy track bends left and then right as you near Blind Hall Farm. (You are walking in an easterly direction.) About 400 yards beyond the farm, continue to follow the track as it veers left (north-east), following the Heart of England waymarkers over several fields until you reach Back Lane.

2 Head left down Back Lane for about 400 yards. Now go left through the hedge gap and walk to the field corner and turn left past a small pond, to arrive near some houses in an area called Four Oaks. Bear left and diagonally cross a large cultivated field to go onto the Meriden road once again. Cross the road and walk down the waymarked driveway opposite (to the right of Wilmcot Cottage). Go through a gateway onto farmland. Walk on the clear footpath to the right of the hedge, with a clear view of Home Farm to the left, and then diagonally across a very large cultivated field. In about 625 yards, you will reach the corner of Mercote Hall Lane. Turn left (west) and stroll along the quiet lane for about half a mile, passing Park Farm. Continue along the lane past the large enclosed sand and gravel pit.

3 At the end of the pit area, turn left onto a waymarked footpath by trees, crossing footbridges and then ascending towards Marsh Farm. Just beyond Marsh Farm, turn left along a farm track and walk towards Sixteen Acre Wood, going

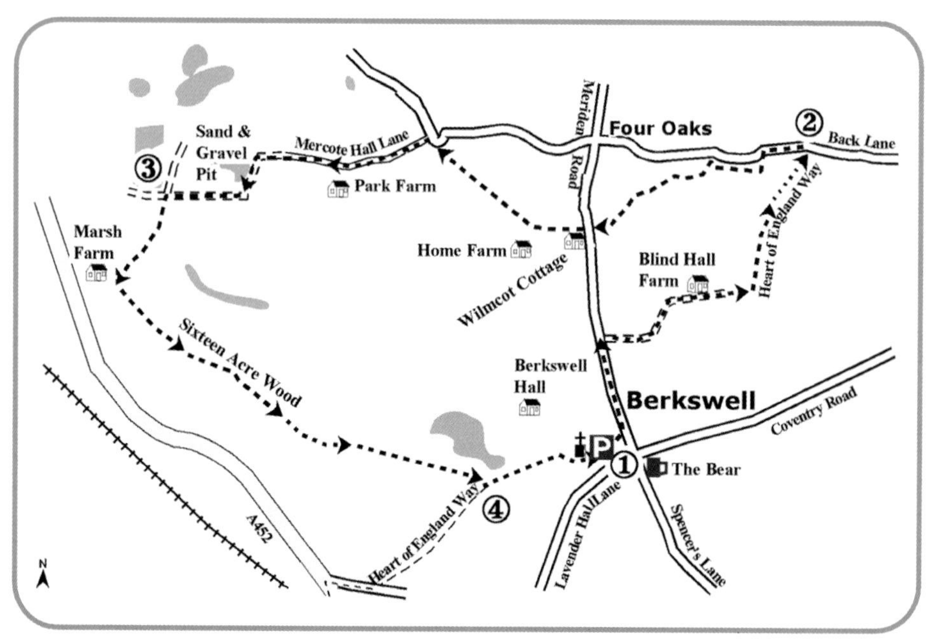

The 12th-century church of St John the Baptist

over a stile into the woodland. Walk along the wood edge track for 700 yards. (This is delightful in autumn, when golden beech leaves cover the ground.) Continue by the hedge and go through a strip of trees into fine parkland. As you walk along the path for the next 650 yards, you will enjoy a magnificent view of Berkswell Hall lake to your left. Soon you enter trees and go through a kissing gate to rejoin the Heart of England Way.

4 Cross the track and bear right over a stile onto a planked area. (Berkswell Hall is clearly visible to your left.) A couple of hand gates lead you back to the village of Berkswell and its wonderful 12th-century church. Inside the church, you will be captivated by the crypt (probably Saxon); enchanted by the 800-year-old stone seats along some of the walls; fascinated by the Russian flag, brought home from the Crimean War; and impressed by the magnificent choir stalls with poppy heads and figures of saints Wulfstan, Dunstan and Chad. Just after going through the church gate, bear left to return to the car park. The Bear Inn is to the right, near the road junction.

Place of Interest

Baddesley Clinton Manor (National Trust), 6 miles south, is a superb 15th-century moated manor house. It is famous for having been a haven for persecuted Catholics: there are no fewer than three priest holes. Telephone: 01564 783294.

Date walk completed:

....

Walk 40 Coventry

The Flying Standard

This is a walking tour of Coventry, taking you past many of the historic buildings of this modern city. At the outset you visit the two cathedrals: the old and the new. The old cathedral was badly damaged during German air raids in 1940 and only ruins remain. Next to this is the new cathedral, where Graham Sutherland's tapestry of Christ in Glory in the Tetramorph dominates its east end. This combination of old and new has made Coventry Cathedral a dynamic centre of worship and mission, a place of pilgrimage, and a frequent venue for national services and television and radio broadcasts. The route takes you round many other important buildings and to the canal basin for a super day out.

Distance: *3 miles*

OS Explorer 221
GR 334793

An easy city stroll

Starting point: The Tourist Information Office in Lychgate cottages (3-5 Priory Row, at the rear of the Flying Standard pub.) Take a booklet explaining the detailed history of each building you will pass by or visit. Telephone: 024 7622 7264 or www.coventry.org for information.

How to get there: Park at one of the park-and-ride car parks and travel into the city by bus, getting off near Cathedral Lanes Shopping Centre.

Housed in a mock medieval building, the **Flying Standard** has a good reputation with visitors and locals alike. You are assured of a warm welcome and good service. A varied menu is available, but the two for £5.75 offer is a favourite with many, and the beer garden is very popular. Real ales include Abbott Ale, Marston's Pedigree and Burton Bitter and Tanglefoot.

Opening times *are from 10 am to 11 pm, Monday to Saturday, and 10 am to 10.30 pm on Sunday. Food is available during opening hours, with last orders taken at 10 pm (9.30 pm on Sundays).*

Telephone: *024 7655 5723.*
Website: *www.jdwetherspoon.co.uk*

The Walk

1 From the information office, walk up Priory Row, turn right along Cuckoo Lane, and then go left between the new and the old cathedrals. Walk back up to Cuckoo Lane; then turn left and left again, down Bayley Lane. (Here you can visit St Mary's Guildhall; dating from the 14th century, it boasts one of the finest great halls in England.) Continue down Bayley Lane into Earl Street. Turn left and cross over Jordan Well at the pedestrian crossing. Then head right down Whitefriars Street. At the bottom of the street, turn right along Whitefriars Lane and stroll beneath Whitefriars Gateway, the remains of a Carmelite friary founded in 1342. Go right along Park Street; then go left along St John's Street to Little Park Street, passing the police station on the corner. Turn right along Little Park Street and then go left over the pedestrian crossing in front of the Tudor-style Council House, which was built between 1913 and 1917, and has a corner clock with statues of Godiva, Leofric and Justice. Head left along High Street, past Cathedral Lanes Shopping Centre, to see the statue of Lady Godiva. It was made by Sir William Reid Dick and unveiled in October 1949 – probably the only naked lady you will see in Coventry!

Now retrace your steps towards High Street, and go right into Greyfriars Lane.

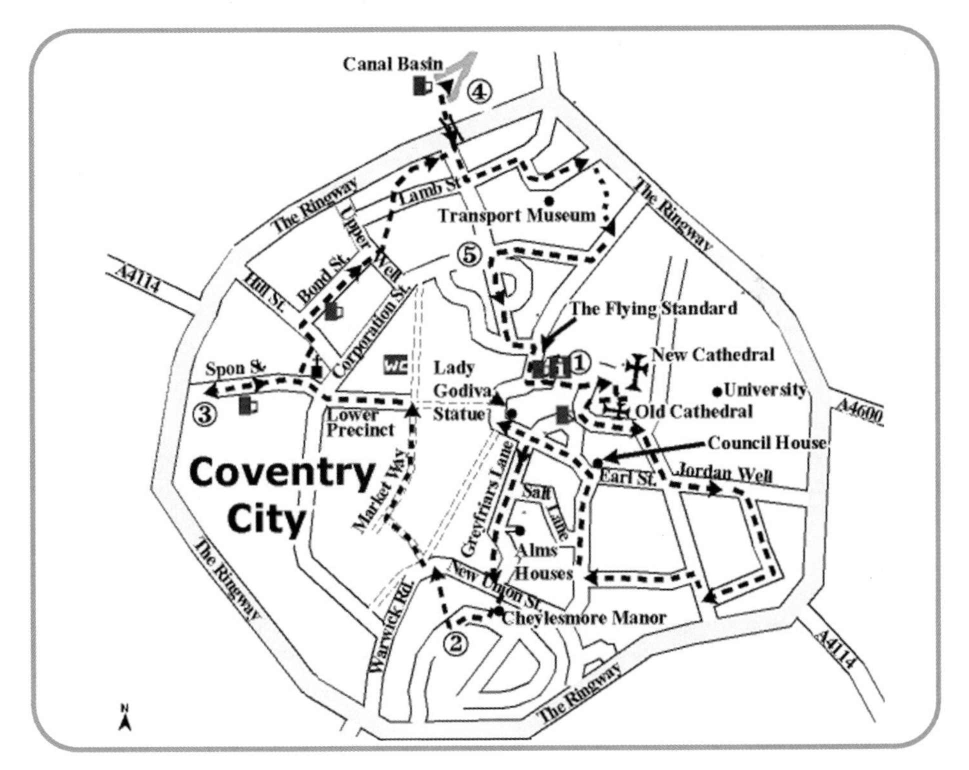

Just beyond Salt Lane is the Ford's Hospital and its wonderful old almshouses, that were badly bombed in 1940. Continue along Greyfriars Lane, walking on the pathway to the right of the impressive 230 ft Greyfriars spire – this is all that remains of 14th-century Christ Church – to arrive in New Union Street. Cross the street and go through the archway to Cheylesmore Manor. (Sadly, the gatehouse is all that remains of the manor of the Earl of Chester.) Soon you arrive at Manor House Drive, where you go right. As you near the corner of the road, go right, down a 'no entry' road, to arrive in Warwick Row and the Quadrant.

❷ Cross Warwick Row and Warwick Road and head into Shelton Square. Bear right and continue along Market Way to reach the main shopping centre. At the central fountain, go left down Lower Precinct, passing the usual high street stores. At the traffic island by St John's church, cross the road to see the fine medieval buildings in Spon Street.

❸ When you reach the end of the street, turn round and retrace your steps to the traffic island. Go left just before the church, passing the buildings of Old Bablake School – founded in 1560 for the education of the poor boys of Coventry – on your way to Hill Street, where you turn left. Bear right along Bond Street, cross over Upper Well Street, and then cross Lamb Street, walking on the footpath that leads towards the canal basin. Cross the footbridge over the ringway to see the Y-shaped terminus, canal warehouses, coal vaults and a fine canal house.

Coventry Cathedral sits alongside the ruins of the old one

❹ Retrace your steps over the footbridge and go down Bishop Street. Head left along Tower Street; then turn right down Cook Street to visit the Museum of British Road Transport. After going beneath Cook Street's 15th-century gateway, one of twelve around the city, go right and stroll through Lady Herbert's Garden to reach Hales Street by Swanswell (priory) Gate that is likely to have been a private entrance into St Mary's Priory. Go right along Hales Street to a road junction.

❺ Turn left and stroll up The Burges. At its end, bear left into Ironmonger Row, and cross the road. Turn right and then left. The Flying Standard is on the left, in Trinity Street.

Place of Interest
Warwick Castle, 11 miles south, is an amazing medieval castle. Telephone: 01926 496277.

Date walk completed:

....